The –
Self-Alignment
Method

Crafting a Life of Harmony and Purpose

By

ANTHONY EMILO

THE SELF-ALIGNMENT METHOD

Crafting a Life of Harmony and Purpose

Copyright© 2024, Anthony Emilo

All rights reserved. No part of this publication may be reproduced, distributed, or transmitted in any form or by any means, including photocopying, recording, or other electronic or mechanical methods, without the prior written permission of the author, except in the case of brief quotations embodied in critical reviews and certain other noncommercial uses permitted by copyright law.

Publisher's Contact

Published by Anthony Emilo
Mightywellness.us
Hello@Mightywellness.us

Adele Wiejaczka (www.livelargedesign.com)
Editing done by Clara Abigail
Formatted by Saqib Arshad (www.24hrpublishing.com)

First Edition

ISBN: 979-8-218-43587-5

Disclaimer

This book is a nonfiction work based on the author's experiences, research, and insights in the field of health and wellness. While the author has made every effort to ensure the accuracy and efficacy of the information provided, it should not be seen as professional medical, psychological, or psychiatric advice. Readers are encouraged to consult with qualified healthcare professionals before engaging in any practices discussed in this book, especially if they have existing medical conditions, are pregnant, or have a history of trauma.

Shadow work can be a powerful tool for personal growth but may also lead to the resurfacing of past traumas. If you are dealing with trauma or if engaging in shadow work triggers distressing emotions or memories, seeking professional support is strongly advised. The safety and well-being of the reader are of utmost importance.

Breathwork is a powerful practice that can offer profound benefits for relaxation, stress relief, and personal growth. However, it is crucial to approach these exercises with caution. They should never be performed while driving, operating machinery, swimming, or in any other situations where altered consciousness could lead to injury. Always practice in a safe, stationary environment.

Additionally, the author makes no guarantees regarding the specific outcomes that may be achieved from applying the strategies and insights shared within these pages. Personal development is a deeply individual process, and results can vary widely among individuals. Success in personal growth, like any other endeavor, requires commitment, effort, and sometimes, facing personal challenges and discomfort. The stories and case studies mentioned in this book are examples of what has been achieved by some individuals and may not reflect everyone's experience.

This book is a tribute to you,
the mentors, the friends, the family, and even the
strangers who have unknowingly steered me towards
paths of discovery and growth.

THANK YOU.

Contents

CHAPTER 09: Shadow Work   97

CHAPTER 10: Energy Work - Balancing and Nurturing Your Inner Self   111

PART

How'd We Get Here?

To live is the rarest thing in the world. Most people exist, that is all.

- OSCAR WILDE

01

Living in Alignment

I'd like to paint you a picture of how I came to develop the Self-Alignment method.

I first started using many of the practices I will outline in this book well over a decade ago. At the time, I was in my late teens and severely depressed. I could see all the darkness being presented to the masses within the fear-based culture, media, and politics of the Western world. The "conspiracy theories" I followed also brought me worry. I was far too focused on these issues, and I was not living in alignment. In fact, I was consistently choosing actions that went against what I wanted to do. Due to my fearful and anxious mindset, I would either take minimal action or worry all day about the action I wanted to take, most often settling on inaction.

I was someone who couldn't possibly believe he could live the life he wanted. Negative perspectives of how the world works and worries for how my own life would end up left me feeling perpetually unlucky. I faced difficulty finding meaningful relationships, struggles obtaining money or following through with my own promises. I bought into the narrative of *"that's just who I am."* So, I constantly considered how much easier it would be to not exist.

But somehow, through all of this, I always had a grand idea of what I *could* be or become. As a kid I watched documentaries like *Super Size Me* and *Zeitgeist,* which led to mistrust in the big industries. I saw my family & friends using commonly accepted interventions such as prescribed anti-depressants or using alcohol as coping mechanisms, and that never sat right with me. I knew the way forward wasn't going to be the typical path. I didn't feel I needed a degree to learn or be successful. I decided to forge my own path, heal my traumas, and eventually offer a hand-up by sharing my story with others. And heck, even *that* gave me anxiety.

Fortunately, I had a spark for finding **more**. I knew there was knowledge that would allow me to change and make room for the truly divine human I always was. I searched endlessly, consuming many self-help and mindset ideologies. I resonated greatly with spiritual information from Eastern traditions and ancient wisdom. It was information for advancing my own consciousness. I developed a love for meditation, breathwork, energy work, and divination, along with practical information about becoming my own boss, being an entrepreneur, and dealing with anxiety/depression. I found by learning from every source I could, I was able to make sense of the world and move forward in a way that aligned with what I truly saw within.

With the Self-Alignment method, I can handle life's challenges, from business hiccups, family dynamics to internal blockages. I'm able to more easily regulate my emotions and catch myself when negatively looping. Instead of giving in to limiting beliefs, I can break them down to their core and reshape my thoughts to better serve me. Moreover, when I make decisions that, in hindsight, are not the best, I can use non-judgmental discernment and self-compassion to move forward, rather than feeling down.

After all these years, I am happy to share the exact methods that have brought me to this point and worked well for those I've worked with. Rather than sending you on your own unguided, decade-long journey, I've put together a field guide with the foundational knowledge I've acquired that can help anyone become re-aligned with their life purpose. Beyond living in alignment, you will learn how to cultivate a powerful mindset and gain spiritual knowledge to help you through any situation. You will uncover the gifts in every challenge and push yourself further into the being *you* were meant to become.

Although the techniques are simple enough, the challenge will come from working with yourself. We often have everything we need, but what stops us is *us*. Yes, many of us are filled with limiting beliefs troubled by a problematic past or stuck in patterns that no longer serve us. Childhood traumas bleed into our daily lives all while we fear that these things are *us*. But the reality is, they are not. They are simply patterns that we've allowed to perpetuate. With the right tools, you can heal from and overcome these difficulties, and deal with any situation that may arise.

Again, we are *not* our baggage. Those struggles push us into "being" and prepare us for the voyage of life. When we peel back those layers of hurt, we see and become the person we want to be, in our highest form. I believe that is the purpose for all of us in this life. My own life path is meant for holding space and guiding others to shine their unique light. To live in a place of love rather than fear and fulfill our purpose on this planet. Whether it is to homestead, start your own festival, be a business-minded entrepreneur or anything else, this is your journey. The Self-Alignment method is the foundation to build yourself up for success, whatever that means to you.

I'd like to share with you a few case studies of how the tools in this method have helped my clients in the past. These will be pseudo names to honor their wish to remain anonymous.

CASE STUDY #1: *Transformed Tracy*

Tracy came to me feeling like many clients I have:

- Feelings of her life never going the way she wanted it to.
- Constantly having negative thoughts about herself and others with plenty of limiting beliefs that fed into her story.
- Knowing she wanted change and how she saw it but not knowing where to start.

Tracy, like many others, was frustrated with her life. She was working at jobs that didn't contribute to who she wanted to be and had troubles in her family of people who weren't supportive. She knew she wanted to live more spiritually, embrace more energetic concepts, and work on her body. That way she could start working closer in relationships as her ancestors did with healing others as a medicine woman.

She knew she needed to start by working on her mindset and losing some weight so she could start feeling better about her body and release the energy being stored from many choices in the past that created her current reality. Tracy found it incredibly difficult to move forward or create lasting changes after living so many years in a state of negativity, anger, and lack. Her struggles became her story, and she knew she needed to reconnect with her purpose.

We started by uncovering exactly how she was feeling and what she saw her current life to be and what she always wanted it to be. We created a crystal-clear vision of the life she wanted to cultivate, including the traits and values of the person she wanted to become.

From here she started to act. Each week she challenged herself not only through action but through the negative mindset she had effortlessly created through the years. She started to be able to put herself in perspective, understand why she held those thoughts in the first place, and feel empowered in allowing herself to dive deeper into who she was and why she had these patterns.

The actions she took became easier. It became easier to set boundaries and deal with the barriers that arose. She started to have better relations with her family, as she was able to navigate through compassion and empathy rather than judgment and anger.

Overall, she built the foundations to being able to choose to be in alignment. To let go of the past and become the person she always had inside her. She was able to finally walk the path towards her highest self and feel fulfilled, not allowing any setbacks to hold her back permanently. To work through her internal challenges and finally cultivate the unique light within her.

CASE STUDY #2: *Doubtful Dan*

Dan's major challenge when he came to me was not being able to take action or commit to the goals, he would set for himself. On top of this, he felt very unconfident in his endeavors and didn't have a very good idea of who he wanted to be or what he was doing in life. He was a fantastic salesman who recently bought a house and had great financial success. Yet, it was hard for him to get anything done or create the space he wanted to have beyond fulfilling his duty at work.

Together, we worked to uncover what his specific limiting beliefs were and why he felt so unconfident in his ability to get anything done, feelings of never having enough time and not committing to what he wanted to create in life.

Dan, using curated practices, worked on learning about himself, the person he felt called to be and the type of experiences he would like to have in life. From there we started to work on committing to his actions, of which he had plenty. We created an action plan starting with mindset work to get to the bottom of what his barriers were, supporting him with tools specific that allowed him to start taking steps in the right direction. Those small steps became fluid strides over the months we worked together, and Dan was able to balance his work life, social life, what he chose to accomplish in his home, and have a better idea of what direction he wanted his life to take him.

CASE STUDY # 3: *Bright-Eyed Betty*

Betty was an individual who had no shortage of dreams, direction, or creativity. By the time we started working together, she was already familiar with many of the concepts that this book covers—though she did not often utilize them. Her main challenges were organizing herself in ways that optimized her abilities and managing stress when it bubbled to the brim.

During our first meeting, it became clear that Betty had an active brain and often considered the outcomes of situations that had not yet been presented to her. I asked Betty questions that brought this tendency to her attention, and she confirmed that this was something that she often found herself doing. We began by working through ways for her to slow down and tackle one challenge at a time.

As we continued our work together, Betty began addressing the way she dealt with (or didn't deal with) her stress. After we identified her triggers and patterns, we discussed ways in which she could prevent herself from getting to that level in the first place. We then created a "exit strategy" for her to refer to whenever she caught herself going down those familiar stress paths.

With these newly developed tools of organization and self-regulation, Betty went on to launch her own business and hit the ground running towards all of her dreams and success.

The one thing that allowed success for myself and for my clients was taking on one hundred percent responsibility for how our lives were going to turn out. This must be one of the most challenging yet beneficial principles to take on in order to create your dream reality. No matter if it was me or my clients, or you, situations arise that require us to tap into our innate wisdom and intuition. Rather than seeing them as a problem we "have" to deal with, it becomes a growth-based opportunity that pushes us further. You *will* face challenges with your internal and external world. What matters is you continue using the principles in this book and those that work for you while being consistent.

If you drop off a few days, choose something that doesn't serve you, give into old patterns—that's okay! Give yourself grace to know that it is alright, don't let it taint the rest of your day, week, or life. Get back up, take accountability, look deep into why that situation happened, and move forward knowing we are imperfect beings. Our ability to learn, let go, and move forward is one of the major concepts my clients and I have used to make massive changes in our lives.

Knowing yourself is the beginning of all wisdom.

- ARISTOTLE

02

Navigating This Book

Here is the basic outline for the flow of material we will cover. First, you will dive into creating a crystal-clear vision for where you are heading, taking account of where you are currently, and what needs to change. Next, we focus on mindset, learning the tools to practice and incorporate into your life for maximum success and balance. Then comes the shadow work—without looking at the parts of us we'd rather not face, we cannot move forward. After that, you will learn about energy work, by considering the full spectrum of our being - using meditation and breathwork to guide us in this journey toward self-alignment. Finally, we will tap into nutrition, fitness, environmental factors, and sleep - without these pillars it's difficult to attain balance.

Overall, you will take on the role of a polymath, a word I recently learned that describes this journey well. A polymath is someone who possesses knowledge of a wide range of subjects. They combine multiple modalities from various frameworks, ideologies, philosophies, arts, and sciences into one. This allows us to gain a higher perspective—a bird's-eye view, so to speak—to tap into which skill(s) you may need to accomplish a feat. It's not always the best practice to be the expert in one specific skillset. Having a depth of knowledge to draw from makes you better equipped.

By implementing the Self-Alignment method, I am hoping that you will see the following improvements in your life:

Harness the ability to think like a polymath; aim to have a basic understanding of the foundations of self-alignment. Discover the reality you always somehow knew you could attain.

Next is to adopt the tools that will help you look within and heal aspects of yourself you didn't know needed to be healed. Gain new perspectives and overall balance to areas of your life calling for your attention.

The most important thing I'd like you to get out of this book is clarity on where you are now versus where you'd like to be. My hope is that by the end, you feel more aligned with your path. This book is a foundational guide to jumpstart you on your path. While this book will not magically teleport you directly to all of your goals, it will bring ease and direction to the process! You, me, and countless others are walking this path. Once started, the happiness and fulfillment from doing the things you want to do becomes easier to tap into.

I understand that this framework could come off as complex at first glance. Each topic we cover will be easy to understand and have simple exercises and knowledge that can be implemented. Also, the Self-Alignment method is highly flexible, allowing you to adjust it to your unique needs.

You may also feel that the time and effort required may be too much for you to commit. These tools are meant to be kept with you for a lifetime. You can choose and pick which ones fit you, but overall, to stay in alignment and go towards your dream reality, it will take time and effort. The journey of evolving as humans is lifelong. Use these tools to help you start a business or start homesteading, deal with internal conflicts, or find clarity in your life. Whatever makes sense for you.

This is a holistic approach, and it is non-linear. We will consider the multiple parts of human life which create the whole. You are not just your organs, you are not just your mind, you are not just your spirit— you are a complex individual with multiple needs that must be met. Like a car with multiple working parts, if you ignore any one part for too long, the whole thing will eventually fail.

If you're seeking additional support, that is precisely where my role at Mighty Wellness comes in! As your guide, I will assist you in carving out your path and maintaining alignment. Instead of dictating how you should live, I will help unveil the parts of yourself capable of addressing your unique needs. You possess all the solutions; I merely facilitate a space for realization, offer tools and knowledge for support, and encourage you to stay true to yourself.

Introduction to Self-Assessment:

Getting Started

The following self-assessments are designed to help you reflect on your current state and readiness for transformation. As you embark on this journey with me, understanding where you're starting from is crucial. Score yourself on a scale of 1-5 for each statement below, where 1 means "This is not at all like me" and 5 means "This describes me exactly."

Assessment Statements:

- I often feel disconnected from my true desires and aspirations due to fear or anxiety.
- I find myself frequently dwelling on the negatives presented by media, politics, or surrounding conversations without seeking solutions.

- The idea of diverging from societal norms (like traditional education or career paths) to forge my own path is both thrilling and terrifying.
- I have experimented with or am open to exploring various self-help and spiritual modalities (e.g., meditation, breathwork) to improve my well-being.
- I recognize the importance of addressing and healing my traumas but feel unsure where to start.
- The concept of becoming a polymath—integrating knowledge from multiple domains to enhance my perspective and solutions—resonates with me.
- I am searching for a holistic approach to align my life but feel overwhelmed by the plethora of information and paths available.
- I believe in the power of self-reflection and the need to confront parts of myself I usually avoid or deny.

Scoring Guide:

- If you scored between 32 and 40: You're highly aware of your inner conflicts and the dissonance between your current state and your potential. You're also open to exploring diverse modalities for transformation. The Self-Alignment method is designed for someone like you, ready to dive deep into self-discovery and healing. Focus on following each section as designed and see what parts you can add into your plan.
- If you scored between 24 and 31: You have a good sense of awareness about your current state and some openness to change. You may have already started exploring various paths but haven't fully committed to any. Concentrate on the Chapter 8 mindset and Chapter 9 shadow work sections to begin addressing the roots of your challenges.

- If you scored between 16 and 23: You're at the beginning of your journey towards self-awareness and might still be figuring out what you truly want. The concept of integrating different modalities might seem daunting, but it's a journey worth embarking on. Start with the basics: mindset Chapter 8 and identifying your direction in Chapter 7.

- If you scored between 8 and 15: You may feel disconnected from the concept of personal transformation or unsure if this path is right for you. That's okay. Consider exploring the initial steps of creating a clear direction for your life in Chapter 7 and gently introduce yourself to the mindset work in Chapter 8. Every journey starts with a single step.

Next Steps:

Regardless of your score, remember that this journey is uniquely yours. The aim is not to achieve perfection overnight but to make consistent, meaningful progress towards aligning with your true self and living a life that resonates with your deepest values. As we move forward, keep an open mind and heart to the possibilities of transformation.

The only journey is the journey within.

- RAINER MARIA RILKE

03

The Key Lessons

Discovering the powerful strategies I'm about to share with you transformed my life during one of its darkest chapters. Throughout my journey, I faced obstacles like depression, self-doubt, and a lack of direction, which inspired me to create the method you're about to learn.

In addition to the strategies for personal growth, it's crucial to recognize the value of balance and take time to recharge. Life isn't solely about pushing yourself to the limit. There's wisdom in stepping back, resting, and reflecting. Embracing moments of stillness allows you to integrate the knowledge and lifestyle changes you're cultivating, fostering a well-rounded and sustainable journey of self-improvement.

And let's be real, it can be exhausting to always be doing deep work.

Through my own path, I've learned many key lessons I'd like to share with you for two reasons:

1. So, you can learn from my mistakes, without the years of challenges.
2. To give you an idea of why I'm so passionate about helping others reignite their fires and align with their true purpose in life.

I'm going to share some personal stories and insights that I believe you'll find incredibly valuable from the perspective of someone who has not only been on this journey for over a decade but will continue this path for the rest of their life.

KEY LESSON 1: *Have a clear vision of where you want to go.*

Throughout my wild ride of self-discovery, I realized how important it is to have a crystal-clear vision of what you want in life. Without a guiding star, it's easy to get lost in the galaxy of information, feel swamped by the endless options we have in our modern society. By having a deep understanding of where you are trying to reach, you will begin to manifest the life you desire.

A clear vision includes more than physical assets; it is also qualities you'd like to adopt for yourself, qualities of who you want to become. Start by asking yourself questions like, "What kind of person do I want to become? What traits and values does this person have? What experiences would I like to have, on personal and professional levels?" By getting down to the nitty gritty, you will have a fully fleshed out picture of exactly what direction you *will* be heading in.

As you explore the different modalities in the book, especially within the vision work chapter (which is all about creating this vision,) remember it is your unique vision that sets your journey apart. Embrace this and stay true to your intuition. Let it be the fire that guides your direction. You don't need to know every step of the way; you only need to know the destination and the path will start to reveal itself as you walk it.

Additionally, by embracing a clear vision of where you would like to end up, your brain will begin to come up with ideas to help you get there. You will be aligning your actions and choices as if you have already accomplished this vision, pulling your destination closer. This is a concept of the Law of Attraction, which I will give more detail about in Part Two of this book.

KEY LESSON 2: *Cultivating a growth-based mindset for personal and professional success.*

As you embark on this journey and clarify your vision, you will undoubtedly encounter obstacles that will test every aspect of your life. You may face disagreement from family or friends, self-doubt fueled by your ego, or setbacks that confront you with fear. By cultivating a positive, growth-oriented mindset, you will be able to view every challenge from a higher perspective and extract unique key lessons, turning setbacks into opportunities. You will start to reflect on your own negative or judgmental thoughts and learn to reframe them in a way that promotes growth, insight, and a path forward that suits you best. One that is not based on fear, judgment, or ego, but guided by your higher wisdom, intuition, and discernment that empowers you.

To develop this growth mindset, you'll first need to understand what it entails and how you can start reframing your thoughts using cognitive behavioral theory. Additionally, we'll explore the science-backed metaphysical aspects of restructuring your subconscious to ensure it remains aligned with your highest purpose and desires.

Moreover, it's crucial to surround yourself with positive influences that encourage your growth, whether it's through books, mentors, or like-minded individuals. Building a support network will help you maintain your growth mindset and stay motivated, even when the going gets tough. By fostering this mindset and leveraging your support system, you'll be better equipped to navigate the challenges that arise and continue making progress toward your goals.

KEY LESSON 3: *Embrace your shadows for personal growth.*

As you delve deeper into your journey, you'll inevitably confront the darker aspects of yourself—your shadows. These shadows embody the repressed emotions, fears, and insecurities that often prevent us from realizing our higher purpose. Becoming aware of and integrating your shadows is a vital step in your personal growth journey, as it was for me.

Acknowledging and addressing these shadows will be challenging, but doing so enables our true authentic and most empowered self to emerge. It also allows us to comprehend the inner workings of the sabotage made by our subconscious and start overcoming them.

To undertake the shadow work covered in Chapter 9, you'll begin by developing self-awareness around these underlying patterns and triggers. Then, you'll nurture self-compassion and self-forgiveness while utilizing various tools to help uncover the roots of your shadows and accept them without judgment or shame.

Keep in mind that shadow work is a lifelong skill that benefits every aspect of your being. I'll introduce some fundamental concepts for you to consider and increase your awareness of. Armed with this information, you can continue exploring shadow work in a way that resonates with you, whether it be seeking a shadow work mentor, working with a therapist, reading about these topics, or pursuing deeper healing. Ultimately, shadow work helps us shed what no longer serves us.

It may also touch on traumas in our life, trigger aspects of ourselves we have a hard time facing and cause some turmoil. If you find that this work is challenging to deal with by yourself. I always recommend you work with a licensed therapist or healthcare professional of your choosing to help guide you.

KEY LESSON 4: *Align daily lifestyle choices with your higher purpose.*

Ultimately, this lesson is about self-care. Often, we make grand plans to pursue a goal (losing weight, starting a side hustle, eating cleaner, etc.) However, while chasing these goals, we continue with our old patterns and ways of thinking. We set ourselves up with unrealistic daily habits, such as creating an extensive morning routine to achieve our desired outcome, only to fall short and eventually feel discouraged and quit. After all, these are promises we're breaking to ourselves.

In this book, we'll define how to implement small, achievable habits that align with our goals. It's not only about doing these things to reach our destination (although that's part of it) but cultivating habits we genuinely enjoy and that align with our desired lifestyle —habits we can maintain for the rest of our lives, not just until we reach our ultimate goal.

To me, self-care means aligning our actions intentionally, keeping promises to ourselves, using self-love and compassion to forgive ourselves when we fall short, and continuing to make progress week after week, whether taking small or big steps.

Aligning our daily choices isn't only about keeping our promises or giving ourselves the space to grow into the person we want to become. It's about recognizing how we treat ourselves, our bodies, and our minds, as well as how we talk to ourselves. One of the most beneficial ways to do this is by examining three major life components: nutrition, movement, and sleep. Without these three pillars, everything becomes much more challenging.

This book will provide the fundamentals of these three areas, allowing you to gain awareness, tools, and practices to help you find balance and start examining your relationship with each component. I don't believe you *must* work out every day, eat one hundred percent clean, and get eight hours of sleep to be successful, but by bringing your awareness to these areas and doing some re-evaluation and cleanup, you can start cultivating practices that make it easier—and feel much better—to achieve your dreams.

Introduction to Self-Assessment:

Embark on this self-assessment with an open heart and mind. It's designed to help you pinpoint where you currently stand on your journey toward personal growth, using the powerful strategies outlined in this chapter. Rate how strongly you agree with each statement on a scale of 1-5, where 1 means "Strongly Disagree" and 5 means "Strongly Agree."

Assessment Statements:

- I have a clear and detailed vision of who I want to become and the life I want to lead.
- I often find myself seeking approval or direction from external sources rather than trusting my own intuition.
- I view challenges and setbacks as opportunities for growth and learning.
- I regularly engage in practices that nurture my growth mindset, such as meditation, journaling, or reading inspirational literature.

⊛ I am aware of my shadows—the parts of myself I prefer not to acknowledge—and actively work on integrating them into my journey of self-discovery.

⊛ I sometimes avoid facing my deeper fears or insecurities, preferring to focus on more superficial personal development goals.

⊛ My daily lifestyle choices (nutrition, movement, sleep) are aligned with my higher purpose and contribute to my overall well-being.

⊛ I struggle to maintain healthy habits consistently, often due to lack of motivation or clarity on how they fit into my broader life goals.

Scoring Guide:

⊛ 32 to 40 points: You're deeply engaged in your journey of personal growth, with a clear vision and a proactive approach to overcoming challenges. Your mindset and daily practices reflect a strong alignment with your higher purpose. To deepen your journey, focus on refining your vision in Chapter 7 and learning to integrate your shadows more fully in Chapter 9.

⊛ 24 to 31 points: You're on your path to personal growth but may encounter obstacles or areas of resistance, particularly around vision clarity and shadow integration. Focus on cultivating a growth mindset in Chapter 8 and aligning your daily habits more closely with your goals.

⊛ 16 to 23 points: You're at the early stages of your personal growth journey, with significant room for developing a clearer vision and embracing the growth mindset. Start by defining your vision more clearly and exploring introductory practices for mindset growth and shadow work. Chapters 8 and 9

⊛ 8 to 15 points: You may feel uncertain or overwhelmed by the concept of personal growth. Begin with small steps: focus on creating your crystal-clear vision in Chapter 7 and utilizing the mindset Chapter 8 to jump start your action. Consider exploring basic practices in nutrition, movement, and sleep to build a foundation for growth which is found in Chapter 11.

Next Steps:

This assessment is a starting point, a mirror reflecting where you currently stand on your journey of transformation. Regardless of your score, the path ahead is rich with potential for growth and discovery. Use the insights gained here as a guide to deepen your engagement with the strategies and practices discussed in this chapter, moving closer to the life you envision for yourself.

Your task is not to seek love, but merely to seek and find all the barriers within yourself that you have built against it.

- RUMI

04

Unlocking the Big Secret

To achieve personal growth and live a life aligned with your passions and desires, there are many challenges and questions that arise. I've been doing this work for over a decade and felt it necessary to walk through some of these essential questions if you want to get the most value out of this book.

Of course, as you know by now, this isn't a "get aligned quick" scheme. While I provide frameworks, tools and practices that can be incredibly helpful, this doesn't necessarily mean it will be easy. Oftentimes we know a pretty good bit about what we want in life but taking action or diving into the unknown tends to cause us to shy away.

Each individual has different limiting beliefs, reasons, traumas, and patterns in their being that make the journey so very different even if the end result is still the same wanting to find alignment in yourself to pursue your passions (or discover what those passions are).

My end goal is to bring you closer to alignment with whatever your inner light is passionate about and gracefully push you towards it. To help you not avoid but embrace the discomfort of this process, learn solid techniques to give you an alternative perspective and deeper insight into who you are and what steps you can start taking to get there.

With all this comes the first question.

Question #1: Will I be able to show up for myself?

This inevitable question is one of the most pressing challenges I see today and a huge challenge for every individual. Showing up for ourselves doesn't always come naturally or something that is taught to us in grade school. Oftentimes we are constantly doing work for other people, or to survive, for our children, partners, etc. But what happens when we stop and allow the space to be there for ourselves? What does showing up for yourself even mean? It can be such an obscure concept, and I know for me I didn't have a grasp on it at all. I was taking actions through the perception of how I thought my life was supposed to be based on what *other* people told or expected out of me.

A good example of this is thinking that you need a college degree to get an education. There are countless people out there who don't fit well in that environment, they may need to learn from hands-on experiences such as becoming a trade apprentice. There are so many ways for you to learn and gain a solid education for whatever you want in life, and uncovering what works best for you is the key.

One of my favorite quotes, which I may use a few times in this book, is from Tony Robbins, which I will paraphrase here: "We have all these things we 'should' do. You should workout, you should get a nine-to-five, you should go to yoga classes, you should be polite at the dinner party, should, should, should... The last thing you want to do is should all over yourself." What's important is that you're acting on what truly matters to you and shining your unique light in whatever way that means for you. Taking action with passion.

Now, showing up for yourself takes on many forms. It comes in how you talk to yourself. Do you give yourself forgiveness? Love? Do you hype yourself up or congratulate yourselves for everything you've done?

How about any promises you make to yourself—are you following through with them? Do you commit to what you want to create in your life? Are you honoring how you feel and taking the necessary action to care for yourself?

How about exercise? Isn't taking care of your vessel a form of showing up for yourself: giving yourself compassion and love? Isn't coordinating time to do absolutely nothing and relax--do the things you want to do without consequence of how long you've binged-watched Netflix, an act of showing up? Of course, do everything in moderation, as bingeing anything can also cause quite a bit of turmoil, which I'm sure we all understand.

The best part of showing up though, is that it doesn't mean completing some project. It doesn't mean being extremely fit, it doesn't mean forcing yourself to do things you don't want to do. What it means is having compassion and insight to know what you need in your life in the moment and then showing up.

I'll give you two personal examples of this:

One stems from the first time I started going to boot camp classes at a gym nearby. I didn't really want to go, but I have a deep desire to motivate others and myself alongside wanting to see, *truly* see, how I can transform my body to be in its peak performance. So, I can protect my wife and my friends, go on long hikes and perform when I want to. So, what did I do? I went to the class, and that's all I needed to do in order to show up. You make it to the class, the event, wherever you are showing up. If it is too hard and you must stop halfway through, you still showed up.

Showing up means exactly what it is. Focus on showing up, rather than any expectations.

The second example is what a teacher of mine who facilitates ice bath workshops, was preaching to us as we were about to go inside the bath. By being at the event, you won. By getting into the ice bath, you've doubled down and won again. If you can't stay the two minutes in, it doesn't matter, as that's extra credit at this point. Getting up, getting uncomfortable, and doing the best you can is showing up for yourself.

By showing up, you allow the unknown to enter. You allow yourself the space to take that class, get into the ice bath. You remove the expectation that *I must meditate for the whole twenty minutes. I must be in the ice bath for the full two minutes...*

No, you don't! You only have to show up, my friends. In this book I only ask you to follow along with the framework, do the activities, and take the pieces of wisdom that work for you. By showing up in this way, you are taking actions to commit to your own journey of improvement.

Reading this book is an act of showing up for yourself. Once you embrace this concept, magic will start to work its way through you and your life. I guarantee that.

Question #2: How do I know this will work for me?

If you are someone who struggles with getting things started, knowing what you want or where to go next, then I'm sure you've already sought out quite a bit of information on improving these traits of yours. Maybe you've read many of these books without following through with action. Perhaps negative thoughts have gotten the better of you by making you feel as though you are not doing enough. So how is *this* book any different?

The best part about the Self-Alignment method is that it isn't some super-secret new method devised by being a divine guru. These are practical, actionable steps that will give you deeper insight into yourself. You will be given many tools, and even if only one sticks for you, that is enough to bring change into your life.

You know yourself best, right? You know the negative patterns that are no longer serving you to some extent. You know how you feel and how your life may not match what you want for it. Otherwise, you likely wouldn't be reading a book seeking to align yourself with your passions and living a fulfilling lifestyle.

The hardest part is always getting the wheels turning, and this book will gas you up to do just that.

Question #3: Can I be honest and open with myself?

This is a question but also quite the challenge itself. To me, this was presented in my earlier days of going to college, on track with a finance major to then transition into my own wealth management company. I felt I had to go to college. It was simply the only way, and my mentor at the time heavily encouraged it; otherwise, they wouldn't mentor me anymore.

At that time, I still knew in my heart that there are many ways to gain an education, but if I wanted to go down this path, I had to start here. Go to college, transfer to a good university, go into wealth management, and I could finally be financially free. Allegedly, only then could I start to do the things I really wanted to do. You may have had a similar experience. Each time I went to class, I realized I hated finance. I did everything in my power to stay, but my grades started to fall, and my ego screamed at me for being a failure, unable to achieve what was meant for me.

Sometime after I dropped all my classes, I was in a peak of depression. I did some real soul searching and realized some problems. This path seemed safe and tidy; it was the easier choice for my ego. But when I truly felt what it was like to live in that environment, it was almost like a piece of my soul was dying. Was that truly my path? No, it wasn't. I was denying all the red flags—my feelings and intuition—to force my way down a path because it was the only thing I knew. I wasn't honest with myself.

A huge section in this book is looking at your life and deciding if it's actually what you want. In my heart I wanted to help people, lecture my truths, and give others the tools to help them embrace and expand their unique light (alongside spreading my wild and New Age hippie woo-woo ideas). Yet at that time, I completely shut it down for being too fearful of what that meant. *Oh crap, I'll have to stand in front of people! I'll have to change my whole career, tell my parents I'm going to be working in this fashion,* which to them meant I was essentially going to be a failure. (They are more accepting now as I embraced my truth and went with it.) I had to build the confidence to follow through with what I was actually called to do.

I was going to say take my word for it, but don't. When you start to follow your path unapologetically and truly pursue it to the best of your abilities, it won't matter what anyone says or thinks—you will be in bliss. Challenge whatever the norms are in your environment but work happily with a full heart whether or not you achieve your big dreams--because you will be putting in the work to truly create the life you desire. At the end of the day...isn't that what we all want? To live a life that we love?

Question #4: Are you taking personal responsibility for your life and actions?

Taking responsibility for your life presents a significant challenge, yet it is a necessary step towards actively shaping your existence. Many people feel trapped or frustrated, believing their life circumstances are beyond their control. However, a crucial part of personal growth and transformation involves taking charge of one's own life. This entails recognizing that you can shape your own experiences and emotions and acknowledge your power to affect changes in your life.

This lesson is repeatedly emphasized in self-help books, courses, lectures, and teachings. Without embracing this principle, you may perceive life as something that merely happens to you, leading you to surrender your inherent power, allowing it to be exploited by others. When you abdicate responsibility for your life and fail to choose your own path, you become susceptible to the whims of others, who might steer you onto a course you never wished to travel.

In my younger years, I succumbed to a victim mentality. I thought my physical appearance and speech impediment made me unlikable. I believed that girls couldn't possibly be interested in someone like me. I was too embarrassed to share my intuition, knowledge, and authentic self because I was living in fear, which I had created through my victim mindset. Now, as a co-creator of reality, I realized that I had been creating from a place of fear. Manifestation requires action, turning the intangible—thoughts, visions, dreams, etc.—into reality. However, my victim-oriented mentality distorted my reality. While this perspective is valid, it is far from ideal.

By taking responsibility for your life, you honor your divine self and recognize your power to create and live the life you desire. This process involves aligning your clear vision with your thoughts, emotions, and actions, and then embarking on your journey. The upcoming chapters on envisioning your ideal self and mindset will delve deeper into taking responsibility and utilizing this to manifest your highest intentions. By learning to take charge of your life, you will start witnessing the magic that unfolds within you.

"

The significant problems we face cannot be solved at the same level of thinking we were at when we created them.

- ALBERT EINSTEIN

05

Proposing A New Multidimensional Path

On the journey of self-growth and discovery, you'll inevitably stumble upon a plethora of self-help materials. From every corner, there seems to be a novel method to change habits, uncover hidden passions, or assume greater responsibility for your life. Often, I find myself adrift in a sea of conflicting statements and viewpoints that offer little understanding of life's multifaceted nature.

Not only do we have the privilege of navigating this information overload, but we also have the task of discerning what works best for us. In a world where everyone is peddling their secret "hack" to exponentially improve your career, health, relationships, etc, it can be challenging to separate genuine wisdom from nonsense.

I've witnessed everything from pushing emotions out of mind to achieve one's goals, to the opposite approach; sitting with your emotions, understanding them, allowing them to flow, and then moving forward.

The problem is that most advice proposes a simplistic one-size-fits-all solution. These solutions often overlook life's myriad dimensions, focusing on one specific area from one specific viewpoint.

Growth, however, requires more than one perspective—it even requires more than our own. A single viewpoint lacks clarity, options, and understanding. Our experiences are limited to our lives and the lessons we've drawn from them, but even then, we don't always adopt a learning mindset from our experiences.

An example of how I approach this is by convening my "war council" whenever I encounter a problem. I discuss my concerns with my trusted advisors—parents, siblings, partner, coaches, friends—and each provides a unique approach, perspective, and understanding of the problem. Through their collective wisdom, I gain clarity and am able to move forward with a well-rounded approach.

My method offers exactly that. Rather than a single perspective, it provides a diverse array of knowledge built from multiple viewpoints, equipping you with the tools and wisdom to navigate your current circumstances. A crucial aspect of this is understanding yourself well enough to apply these tools effectively.

And so, I extend an invitation for you to embark on this transformational journey. This isn't a path of quick fixes or superficial solutions. It's an invitation to unravel the complexities within you, to appreciate your unique attributes, and to foster a compassionate relationship with yourself and the light you bring to the world. Rest assured; you won't walk this path alone. I am here as a guide, a friend, and a fellow imperfect human being, walking each step side by side with you.

Let's reclaim our lives together, thriving and moving forward in alignment, with passion, and with love.

PART

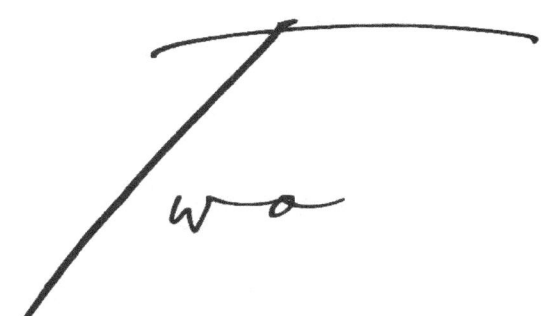

Two

Self-Alignment Method

You have power over your mind - not outside events. Realize this, and you will find strength.

- MARCUS AURELIUS

CHAPTER
06

Reclaiming Your Power

Before we delve into the core of this section—aligning with your goals and acquiring the necessary tools to reach them—I want to introduce you to a straightforward formula I picked up from Jack Canfield's course "Train the Trainer"

E + R = O

(Event + Response = Outcome)

This formula is a core mechanism and mindset I'd like you to consider adopting and playing around with. It is said that when an event happens, coupled with your response to this event, it will manifest a specific outcome.

An example of this could be often arriving late to work. Today you came in about fifteen minutes late, and your manager is in front of you wanting an explanation. Your excuses for being late will dictate a specific outcome.

The event being: Your manager wants you to explain why you're late today.

Your response: "Oh, my engine wouldn't start."

Outcome: The manager may believe you're making things up, knowing you're always late to work, questioning your ability to be a part of the company.

Your response: "Oh, my alarm didn't go off this morning. I'm sorry!"

Outcome: The manager may question your reliability and foresee potential issues down the line. If it's a pattern, this could affect their perception of your professionalism and commitment to the role.

Or you could try a different response, such as:

Your response: "You know, I didn't give myself enough time to get ready, and I understand I've been late in the past. I apologize, and I'll make an effort to get things in order."

Outcome: Your manager appreciates the accountability, giving an opportunity to change their perception and improve the situation.

Your sincerity in taking responsibility for your actions and proposing solutions to improve can significantly impact the outcome. You can recognize that how you choose to respond to the situation can have drastically different results.

We have an absolute responsibility to do our best to take accountability and respond in a way that gives us the most likely outcome for what we want.

If you're in an argument with your partner or someone close to you, you could respond in anger. Yelling, fighting, calling each other names, or pointing out their faults. Blaming them for the situation, which will lead to a plethora of many negative outcomes. You could instead understand that you're angry, take a moment to do something that helps you become grounded or heart-centered, and then explain to them what's going on, what hurt you, or what the problem is in a more compassionate way.

The latter will provide a better environment to create an outcome where you are heard, understood, and can move forward compared to the former, which may build resentment and more negative feelings toward that person.

Now, does this mean you have to perfectly respond every day to every single problem? No, you are not perfect, and neither is anyone else. The idea behind this is to know in your mind that *you* have the power to choose how you respond, which in turn more greatly manifests an outcome that is aligned with your wants.

I'd also like to briefly mention that all outcomes, even if you give a response that honors you authentically and responsibly, may not be what you wanted. For example, expressing to someone what you need in a friendship. This may show you that they aren't fit to be your friend and you lose them as a consequence. Yet, you also learned what qualities you'd enjoy in friendships and honored your authenticity, allowing yourself to connect to others in the future in a way that best suits you.

This all builds up into the largest part, which is that you are accountable for your choices, actions, and responses to everything. The reason why your life is the way it is, is because of the collective choices that you've made up until this point. Without having this understanding, it will be incredibly difficult to reach a growth-based mindset.

Does this mean you weren't dealt a crappy hand of cards? Does this mean you don't have any trauma? Parents who didn't teach you correctly? A teacher who is so anal no one passes their class? A mind that constantly tells you you're not enough? Absolutely not. We only have what we've experienced through our environment.

Yet, when you are on a journey of self-growth, you recognize that the past cannot be changed. We can give it a good hard look and choose to respond differently, respond in a way that allows us to see the lessons hidden in the pain and discomfort.

For us to reclaim our power, we must take responsibility for everything in our lives. We must do our best to honor our authenticity, speak with intention to ourselves and others, and most importantly, have compassion when it doesn't always go our way.

You have the power. You make the choices. You are a co-creator of your reality.

A clear vision helps give us a glimpse of who you are becoming and what that life looks like.

07

Creating a Crystal-Clear Vision

One of the first steps you need to take on any endeavor is thinking about what you'd like the outcome to be. You need to literally imagine a vision within your mind and bring it from this ethereal realm to the physical. Almost everything we see in our lives when we look around was created from that—a thought, dream, or vision.

The importance of having a clear vision is that it gives us a roadmap of where you are headed and will keep you focused on your aspirations. When this vision is aligned with your passions it will act as a GPS that guides you toward your dream, helping you set sights on what truly matters.

We will explore what makes you tick, what fires up your passions, breaking free from what limitations that may be holding you back. We will uncover how our thoughts shape our world and how you're the captain of your ship.

We're going to be using some cool techniques to make this happen—techniques that will help expand your toolset, tap into your imagination, intuition, and internal wisdom. We are going to journal our way into clarity, visualize our dreams coming true, and practice some calming breathwork and meditation that will help align you with your vision in further chapters.

But here's the thing: you don't need to have all the answers right away, and you won't need to be a mindful master to utilize any of these activities. We're not about perfection; we're about progress. You won't need to know how to go from point A to B, only get a deep understanding of where your end point is, and as you walk the path you will uncover how to get there. Find happiness in the journey, for you will be taking actions toward your dreams, which pulls your vision closer every day.

Uncovering Your Desires and Passions

Our passions and dreams serve as the very core of our existence. It is the driving force that propels us forward even when confronted with life's challenges. But why is it so important to align ourselves with them?

It creates an authentic self-expression. This authenticity acts as a beacon which guides us towards the choices and experiences that we truly resonate with. Living in alignment with our passions ensures that every step we take will be infused with a greater purpose.

Not only will we be in alignment with what we truly desire, but the act of creating an inner experience, fueled by deep emotions is a requirement for opportunities to arise in your favor. I truly believe the universe will provide you with an exact match of your inner environment. Whether that is through mystical means or simply focusing on your passions, it allows your brain to see opportunities it otherwise wouldn't be able to see.

Understanding our true dreams and passions without letting anything tie us down is key. By moving beyond our own doubts, past errors, and the pressures from those around us, we can discover what we genuinely want deep down.

Let me paint a picture from my past to explain. Back in 2020, life threw me a curveball. I was let go from my job because of the Covid situation. To make things more challenging, on that very day, I got news that my grandmother had been injured and my grandfather was hospitalized. With my job gone, I had an opportunity to step in and assist. Initially, it was about simple tasks: looking after the house, feeding the dogs. But as days turned into weeks, it became clear that my grandmother would need more long-term support. So, we made a plan: I'd move in and take care of her with my fiancée at the time.

During that year, living at my grandmother's, I had ample time to think and reflect. I had always been fascinated by motivational speakers like Tony Robbins. The way they moved people, the way they inspired others; I felt a similar calling. But a swarm of doubts buzzed around my head. Would my family laugh off this aspiration? Did I have what it takes? Despite these worries, a part of me, a voice deep inside, constantly nudged me towards this path. It reminded me of my longing to help and inspire others.

In a stroke of "luck," my wife introduced me to a friend of hers who was a life coach. Conversations with her, and a few more people she recommended, brought clarity. And then, I made a bold move. I used my savings to enroll in a coaching program. It felt like I was placing a bet on myself. The journey was as exciting as it was challenging. I relished every moment, from the lessons I learned to the practice sessions with people. Every day, I felt more aligned with my calling. Yes, there were hurdles and a lot to grasp, but I knew with dedication and persistence, I'd become the coach my heart desired to be.

I had to let go of my inner fears to pursue a career and life that makes me feel fulfilled, excited, and one where I get to serve others.

There are a variety of ways that you can go about uncovering your desires and passions, which I will list below. I invite you to choose the ones that call to you.

Before any reflection, I find it best to center yourself through being in a quiet, distraction-free environment.

A basic centering practice you can use is box breathing: breathe in for five to seven seconds, hold for five to seven seconds, breathe out for five to seven seconds, hold for five to seven seconds, and repeat the cycle as needed. (try 3-5 cycles)

Author's Note: More details on meditation and breathwork can be found in Chapter 10.

Set your intention for the session and practice whichever of these techniques work best for you.

Journaling:

Write down everything you want without holding yourself back and most importantly, without judgment. Over time, you will notice patterns, and your desires will become clearer.

If you're having a difficult time knowing what you're passionate about or what you desire, you can also write down all the experiences you would like to have and work your way backwards. Once you have your experiences down, why do you want those experiences? Get as deep as you can to uncover the core desire.

Furthermore, you can reverse engineer this question by writing down exactly what you do *not* want. By having a list of everything you no longer want in your life or want to move beyond, you can then reverse them and write down what you do want. (Bonus points if you burn that paper with your intention set on releasing what no longer serves you.)

For example:

I dislike having friends who push me aside and don't value what I have to offer.

The reverse: I want high-quality relationships with individuals who care about me.

I dislike how I stop myself from sharing about topics I care so much about, in fear of judgment.

The reverse: I will speak my truth authentically.

Limitation Listing:

Write down all the external constraints you feel are holding you back from pursuing your dreams. This could be societal expectations, family pressures, financial concerns, etc. Next, write down next to these constraints why they shouldn't influence your desires.

Self-Reflection Session:

Sit down for ten to twenty minutes, ideally in a location without distractions and is quiet. Take some deep breaths and ask yourself, "What do I truly desire?" Let your mind wander without judgment.

You could also think about a time when you were truly passionate about something specific and reflect on what about it made you feel those deep emotions.

Think of what you enjoy most! When were you at your happiest? What activities do you enjoy? Ever reach a flow state during an activity? Do you love teaching others things you learn? Maybe you've always had a desire to do something but have been too fearful to act?

Our curiosities, what we gravitate towards, things that create passion within us, books we enjoy reading, media we enjoy consuming—they all have a specific spark that aligns with our desires and can give us clues on what we enjoy and how we can pursue it.

⊛ *The "Why" Chain:*

Method: Ask yourself, "What do I want?" Once you have an answer, ask, "Why do I want it?" Repeat this until you get to the core of your desires.

By taking time to write down and reflect on your passions, desires, and experiences you'd like to have, or what you'd rather let go of in your life, you will come out of this with a deeper understanding of the type of vision you're starting to create.

The goal here is to figure out what you value, desire, and want to experience so you can take those deeper emotions and apply them to your vision.

Defining Your Vision

Defining your vision is a huge step into creating a crystal-clear vision, and here's why:

"Where attention goes, energy flows."

At the heart of manifestation is the power of intention. A clear vision allows a distinct direction for this intention. There is a huge difference between "wanting success" versus having an extremely detailed vision such as running a thriving bakery that uses high-quality ingredients, teaches baking classes to the local community, and can support you financially. The more specific you are, the more potent your intention will be.

A well-defined vision also evokes strong emotions. These emotions help fuel the manifestation process. When you visualize a particular outcome that is aligned with joy, gratitude, and excitement, it aligns your vibrational frequency with that desired outcome, a topic we will dive deeper into in later chapters.

A clear vision will guide your actions and serve as a roadmap. It creates a greater likelihood to make decisions that are aligned with your goals that lead you closer to that reality.

A lack of a vision or vagueness creates uncertainty of the direction you will be going. With a clear vision, you can commit to the process, reducing the need to second-guess yourself.

While pursuing your goals will not be an easy task, A clear vision acts as an anchor, keeping us grounded, and reminds us of the direction we are going in regardless of what the external factors are.

Allow your vision to spark your fire and bring excitement into the mundane. If it isn't exciting, it's not big enough.

You do not need to know every step of how you will achieve this. You only need to know where you are currently at and where you would like to be. The pieces start to fall together as you walk with intention on this journey, and you'll find that the goal itself isn't as far off as you may have thought.

The Power of Visualization

Our mind is an incredible tool that can relive our past, experience our future, and shape our destiny. One of the most potent techniques we can use is visualization. This isn't only a practice of those who are daydreaming but one that is employed by the world's most successful individuals. It may be an athlete preparing for a competition, professionals gearing up to give a presentation, artists visualizing their next project or even engineers putting together the pieces of their invention.

One interesting aspect found in neuroscience research is that our brain has an incredibly hard time distinguishing what is a vividly imagined experience or a real one (Dijkstra & Fleming, 2023). When we vividly imagine something, we are activating the same neural pathways as if we were doing it in reality. For instance, an athlete who visualizes a perfect performance, the brain starts to use the exact same sequences as it would during the actual event. Priming it for optimal results.

A huge aspect to this phenomenon is the Reticular Activating System (RAS) as a cluster of cells at the base of our brainstem. While it has many functions, in short, the RAS acts as a filter to determine which sensory information is prioritized in our conscious awareness. When you visualize your goals or vision, you are preparing the RAS to notice opportunities, resources, and information aligned with that vision. Have you ever learned a new word and suddenly, it's popping up everywhere you look? Or potentially decide on a car and start to see the same model all around you? That is the RAS in work.

Visualization serves as a rehearsal. The more you practice, the more you are priming your brain to recognize the pathways and achieve it. It's like building a mental muscle. The more you practice, the more aligned your brain will be towards recognizing the opportunities and resources aligned with your vision.

Before hopping into defining your vision, I'd invite you to go over some of these practical tips I've learned along the way that will help make the visualization process more effective:

- Quiet space - A quiet space free from distractions will allow you to become fully immersed in the practice.
- Focused breathing - Start with deep breaths. This calms the mind and helps prepare it for the visualization journey. Inhale deeply through the nose and exhale through the mouth. (If nose or mouth breathing is difficult for you, any inhale or exhale from your mouth or nose will work.)
- Use all your senses - When you start to visualize the scene in your head, do your best to hear it, feel it, touch it, or even taste it. The more senses you use, the more impactful the result will be.
- Emotionally connect - Connect emotionally with your vision. Feel the gratitude, joy, love, excitement, or any other emotion that may arise once you achieve what you're visualizing.
- Daily practice - The more you visualize, the better you'll get at it. Don't expect it to be perfect, and it may even be uncomfortable at first.
- Use visual aids - Vision boards, pictures, posters, or any other tangible items serve as an effective way to keep your vision in mind. If it's more difficult to visualize in your head, this is a perfect way to see it right in front of you. It acts as a reminder and gets the creative juices flowing.
- Visualize in the first person, as if the outcome of your visualization has already occurred.

  - An example: You made first place in your race. You're sweating, heart pounding. Waves of gratitude and joy run across your whole body. Your friends are cheering you on. You can hear the other runners coming in, the crowd congratulating and celebrating the win.

o Tap into it as if it's actually happening, for your brain, body, and universe have no distinction besides the information you give it, real or not.

Activities

⊛ **Journaling:**

Take a moment to envision your perfect day. Picture every detail from the moment you wake up until you go to bed. When you open your eyes, what do your surroundings look like? Who are you with, if anyone? What activities fill your day? What work or creative projects are you engaged in? How do you feel physically and mentally throughout the day? Write down and describe your ideal day in as much detail as you possibly can and how it aligns with your long-term goals. The more specific, the better.

⊛ **Values Reflection:**

What are your values? Do you stand up for what you believe in? Is family everything? Is being honest and courageous meaningful to you? Write down all the values you're cultivating and attach that to the future you're pulling into the present.

On the flip side, what values do you currently hold that may no longer be serving you? Do you have anything you're looking to release and not come with you onto this journey?

⊛ **Visualization:**

In this practice, rather than describing a perfect day, visualize your future self, living your desired reality. You will close your eyes, take some deep breaths in a comfortable spot, and simply imagine who you are in this future reality. How do you look? How do you feel, mentally and physically? How do you uphold yourself when speaking to yourself, friends, family, or strangers? What have you accomplished so far?

It's important to add in any goals you're working on and as you think about an accomplishment you've completed. Feel the emotions that come from that.

You can take what you've envisioned and write them down in detail, giving you a fuller picture of who you are to become and the type of life that you live.

- ⊚ *Create a Mind Movie* - This is something I picked up from a variety of sources and can be utilized in a few different ways to achieve different outcomes. find images or video clips that align with the desired outcome of your vision. Then you can put them together either on a PowerPoint, iMovie, or other software to create a slideshow. You can include music you enjoy that motivates you. You can add affirmations, quotes etc.

You can also adapt this to be an audio file where you record yourself speaking as if you are in the future, what you've achieved, expressing gratitude and energy for the outcome as if it's already happened. It's an audio letter to yourself from the future.

Once created, you will then watch or listen to this movie every night or as frequently as you can. Preferably in the morning as you wake, or at night before going to bed as that is when your subconscious is open to programming.

> ◎ *Letter from the Future:*
>
> Write yourself a letter from your future self. Thank yourself for all the work you've put in to make your vision a reality. What did you have to do to get here? How did you push yourself? How did you overcome these challenges?
>
> Write as much detail as you like. This will help solidify your vision.

I take the stance that every possibility is already happening. All you're doing is defining your exact desires, passions, and wants for the life you're cultivating. By focusing on these thoughts or using these practices in the present, you're calling out to the future in which it exists and pulling it in the "now moment". Your future self is literally begging and thanking you for putting in the work to allow this beautiful vision to come to fruition.

Each time we focus on it, act with intention and keep on walking. We are pulling our vision closer and closer to the present.

Trusting the Unseen Path

Along this journey, you will find that trusting the unseen path is a theme I'll be bringing along with us. While the unknown may be a challenging aspect of life, it is one that brings out the magic as well. We do not need to know the exact details of how to achieve your vision or dream. The act of focusing on the result as it has already happened alongside crafting the exact outcome you would like for yourself will lead you on a journey to achieve it.

I guarantee by utilizing the activities above, you have already started to come up with ideas that are aligned with that vision and how you could get started. It's not about taking massive leaps or getting rich quick. In essence, you only need to uncover what the next step will be, and frankly I find there are plenty of next steps.

For me, I had to use discernment to figure out which step I wanted to take, rather than not knowing where to go. This made me incredibly indecisive, but once you have a clear vision and know your intention, it becomes much easier to know which way to walk.

Trusting the unclear path is also about surrendering to the flow of life. It doesn't mean giving up or not taking proactive steps towards our goals. Instead, it's about recognizing that we don't have control over everything. By surrendering, we release the stress of needing to know all the answers. We become receptive to guidance, insights, and opportunities that the universe presents.

In the grand scheme of our journey, every step, even the uncertain ones, holds significance. Trusting the path is an invitation to trust ourselves, our capabilities, and the universe's grand design. It's a gentle reminder that even in the midst of ambiguity, we're exactly where we need to be, evolving and aligning closer to our true essence with each step.

Stepping Forward with Clarity

In this chapter, we've talked about the importance of creating a crystal-clear vision that is fueled by your desires and passions. Allowing you to understand the exact intention you have moving forward which creates a perfect roadmap for your choices, actions, and seeing opportunities around you to achieve that vision.

We've uncovered the power of visualization and its importance in creating the outcome we want to have and learned how to use it to craft a clear vision. Throughout the rest of this book, you will find more visualizations and practices that will help you align yourself with this outcome.

I encourage you to continue practicing the activities we've gone over and read or visualize them every day to get the strongest effect. It will stay fresh in your mind and point you in the direction you want to go and give you motivation for the tasks ahead.

Whether you think you can, or you think you can't — you're right.

- HENRY FORD

08

Mindset Frameworks

Now that you have a defined vision, you might be asking, "How do I take action on it?" I mentioned that the most important part is knowing where you are now and having a clear direction you want to head in, while also trusting the unseen path. But challenges will come up.

When you face these challenges with the right mindset, you can not only overcome them more easily but also use them to push you forward, gaining experience and skill, instead of getting held back or stuck.

Mindset is essentially the way we see, interpret, and respond to the world around us. It guides our actions, forms our beliefs, and really determines how we handle daily life, deciding if negative or positive events help us grow or pull us down. Here are some key truths I've discovered:

1. Beliefs shape reality: Our beliefs can either limit us or empower us, and they're directly tied to our choices. If we think we can't do something, often we won't try. But if we believe we can, we'll likely give it a shot and find ways to make it happen.

2. Resilience and adaptability: With a growth mindset, we see challenges as chances to grow, not as insurmountable problems. This kind of thinking builds resilience, helping us recover from setbacks and adapt when needed.

3. Influence on well-being: Our thoughts connect directly to our physical, mental, and spiritual health. A positive mindset can lead to less stress, better health, and a general feeling of contentment. On the other hand, a negative mindset can harm all parts of our well-being, even causing disease.

4. Manifestation: The outside world reflects our inner world. Our thoughts send out vibrations to the universe. When our mindset aligns with our desires, it attracts opportunities, people, and events that match those desires. But a negative mindset can bring negative results or associations.

5. Interpersonal relationships: How we see ourselves and others affects our relationships. A mindset that's open and compassionate can build trust and deepen connections with ourselves and others. The stories we tell ourselves play a big part in how we treat ourselves and those around us. Think about your inner voice. Is it kind? Critical? Negative? These inner thoughts will show in our outer actions.

In the end, our mindset isn't just something that passively affects our lives. It actively shapes our reality, our potential, our experiences, relationships, inner feelings, and even our health. Building a strong, resilient, growth-focused mindset isn't only a tool. It's a life-changing skill that touches every part of our lives, leading us to a truer and satisfying life.

The Pillars of a Powerful Mindset

At the core of personal development is the practice of self-awareness. It is the art of understanding ourselves, which comes with immeasurable wisdom to help us be in alignment with our most authentic self. We will be skipping right past the superficial level and into the depths of our being. We will go through practices that uncover our strengths, weaknesses, emotions, and motivations.

Without having a good understanding of yourself, how can you make changes? After all, in order to create the life, you want, you have to become the person who can achieve it.

Finding Your Strengths

A good place to start is understanding what your strengths are. By recognizing your strengths, you will be able to utilize them in any endeavor that you may encounter. It will help maximize your potential alongside increasing your confidence. For instance, if you have a strong desire to learn, you may find that learning new skills is something you will excel at during your journey. Also to note is that no strength is "fixed"—you can and will always be able to increase your skill level in any strength, task, etc. If you recognize an area as weak, you can take that recognition and then apply it towards practicing that skill.

Activity: Personal Inventory

1. Write down every skill, task, or activity that you believe you're good at, no matter how big or small.
2. For each item, write down a brief moment when you demonstrated that strength.
3. Reflect on how each strength made you feel when exercising it.

Activity: External Input

1. Ask three to five close friends, family members, or colleagues what strengths they see in you.
2. Reflect on your personal inventory. Is there anything they said that matched up? Anything that surprised you?

Activity: Strengths Storytelling

1. Recall a challenging time in your life that you've overcome.
2. Write a brief story about it. How did you overcome it?
3. Identify what strengths you relied upon during this time and how it made you feel to overcome this challenge.

Activity: Strengths Assessment

I highly recommend taking the VIA Character Strengths Survey. It will give you a structured approach and may shine light on areas you may not have known about or give you deeper insight on your own strengths.

In order to get the maximum benefits of how you can use your strengths, I recommend taking everything you've learned about your personal strengths and writing down how you can integrate them into your personal life and towards your vision.

Finding Your Weaknesses

Recognizing weaknesses or outdated beliefs that no longer serve you will be vital in your journey for alignment. This isn't a process in which we self-criticize or focus on a pity party. It is a space of non-judgement and deep reflections that allow us to move forward in a new direction. By understanding what is currently going on in you, negative or positive, you will have a greater idea of the areas you will need to work on.

Oftentimes we already know habits or beliefs that may be making it more difficult to live a life aligned with your desires. I want to note that I'll be giving a deeper look into this topic through looking at our limiting beliefs further into this chapter, alongside the next chapter, which goes into understanding our shadow. It's always important to come into work that deals with our unsightly side in a positive, non-judgmental manner that allows you to see it as something that no longer serves you and can be changed rather than something that is a quality of who you are.

Once you recognize there is a problem, it is no longer a problem. It is a choice. You can continue to choose to repeat these patterns, or you can choose to move beyond them.

Activity: Habit Tracking

1. For one week, write down all the habits from your waking state until you go to sleep.
2. At the end of the week, categorize these habits into "helpful," "neutral," or "no longer serve me."
3. Focusing on the third category of "no longer serve me," ask yourself why you are still holding onto these habits.

Activity: Confronting Avoidance

1. Identify tasks you consistently procrastinate on or avoid.
2. Dive deeper into understanding the "why" behind this avoidance.
3. Oftentimes this can uncover hidden fears, weaknesses, or beliefs that may be harmful to your progress.

Activity: Reverse the weakness!

1. Take all of those habits, what you've been avoiding, weaknesses that you perceive, and create a list of them.
2. Next to any given "weakness," write out the opposite of it or how you would want the new habit to be.

For example:

- Not getting enough sleep - Getting a full eight hours of sleep
- Using alcohol to deal with stress - Using exercise to help alleviate stress
- Finding it difficult to speak your truth - Being able to communicate what you mean

What you're doing is identifying areas that no longer serve you, then identifying what this looks like flipped on its back. That way you can take the positive aspect and use it as a guide for your actions.

Uncovering Our Emotional Landscape

Understanding our emotional landscape can be a powerful indicator of our well-being and provide valuable insight to our reactions. The more data we can collect on ourselves, the more information we will have to understand what's going on.

A remarkably simple exercise you can do is write down your emotions in the morning, afternoon and night. You could use a sad face, neutral face, or happy face to indicate what was going on and write down reasons why you may have felt that way.

Do this for one week and you will have more insight into your patterns and triggers alongside offers a window into your emotional well-being. Again, once we recognize any patterns or potential triggers, we can then choose a different path, rather than stay stuck in the same programmed loop we created for ourselves.

On top of this, when it comes to manifestation, the state that you currently are at is what you will bring towards you. By understanding your emotions, your triggers, and learning how to be in a state of gratitude, joy, love...coupled with your vision, you will allow it to come easier towards you.

Understanding Motivation & Cultivating Discipline

Lastly, understanding your own motivations and the internal fire that drives you will be a huge part of your journey. By knowing your motivations or the "why" behind what you're doing, it can help invigorate you to take intentional action. Although, I want to mention that motivation is fleeting and should not always be relied on.

For instance, many gain motivation at the end of the year when they start to write out their New Year's resolution. As many of us have seen, the gym will be packed with people wanting to better their lives. Yet as the days or weeks go on, only a few stay consistent. This is because motivation fades and it's easy to revert to old comfortable patterns, yet with practicing discipline, you can stay consistent even when your motivation starts to dwindle.

Discipline is a form of self-control. It allows us to enact a behavior regardless of external circumstances. Some people may find this easy, while others may struggle to hold discipline in their life, including myself. At one point or another we have all had challenges that involve discipline. Whether that's being on time, eating food that isn't the best for us, or going out on the town when we have work that needs to be done.

Discipline for me is a lot like showing up. It's showing yourself respect and love to continue going towards your authentic self or vision rather than retreating into the old patterns. Discipline is a skill—it's something we can learn and improve upon. All you need to do is practice.

Embracing Setbacks and Advancing with Discipline

Many people will get caught up and stop putting in the work once they miss a day or two at the gym, fall off a lifestyle change or any other habit they are trying to cultivate. It's important to remember that you are here to walk the path. The end result is a side project of it. Once we fall down, we re-examine in a non-judgmental way what went wrong, then get back to it and try our best to continue forward.

Everyone who succeeds will encounter massive setbacks. The difference is they kept with it.

By combining both a deep motivation that reminds you of your vision and where you are aiming to go, with utilizing discipline to keep you on track even on days that provide you with massive barriers. You will be able to take action on your big leverage tasks quicker and with less fuss.

Discovering Your Why

You may be asking, "How do I gain motivation? How do I practice discipline?"

When it comes to motivation, one of the best things you can do is focus on the whys behind the goal. Simply write out or ponder all the reasons behind the actions you're taking. You also want to make sure that the reason behind the goal is substantial enough to make you motivated. Losing weight or gaining strength may not be enough. Why do you want to lose weight? Is it so your body will have less stress, more mobility, and allow you to play around with your grandchildren or live longer, unlike others who die premature deaths?

Or maybe the reason behind gaining strength is so you can defend your family in case an intruder comes. What if you need to run a long distance with your child on your back? Can you?

Try your best to get into the nitty gritty of your motivation and your goals. Connect to the deeper aspects of what your goal will allow you to do or achieve. Wanting to lose weight is the very surface level of a much deeper area within you.

You can also visualize completing your end goal, feeling all the emotions associated with it. I highly recommend doing this regularly, using your vision that you wrote out. This will keep you focused on the big picture while you start to do things that may not be as enjoyable.

I quite enjoy the process of coaching, but to set up a business, the majority of the time you are actually working on the infrastructure, website, sales, marketing, etc. rather than the service you are wishing to provide. Yet by making it through all these aspects and reminding myself it's so I can follow through on my mission, it becomes easier to accomplish these tasks and find the motivation.

Let's see how the Why Chain can help us with uncovering our motivation in this next activity.

Activity: *The "Why" Chain*

- Write down something you're currently struggling to find motivation for. An example would be going to the gym.
- Then, write down all the reasons why, continuing to get as deep as you can.
- Once you have gotten to the core of your whys, which should be personally meaningful to yourself, visualize yourself accomplishing those whys.
- In our example, this could be visualizing yourself being fit, losing weight, and having more energy to spend with your loved ones. Feeling immense gratitude and pride for what you've accomplished.

Motivation has multiple categories that can define it. I tend to focus on cultivating two of them. Intrinsic motivation occurs when someone generally enjoys what they're doing. They are going on a hike because they enjoy hiking. The next is Identified Regulation. This occurs when we do an activity because we know it will help complete a goal that is meaningful for us, such as going on a hike so we can lose some weight, spend more time outdoors with our family, etc.

By creating as many opportunities as possible to pursue activities that activate your intrinsic motivation alongside reminding yourself of your large goals through focusing on them in a variety of ways, you will help create that inner fire to keep you on track.

When it comes to discipline, it's as simple as doing. *Just Do It!* Yet when it comes down to it, this can be a more difficult process than we think. Aligning your actions with your end goal is the key. If working out is the vessel to achieve your health goal, then creating a plan to become disciplined in it will be easier to accomplish.

If our whys, vision, or actions are not aligned, not big enough, don't excite you...then it's going to be tough to get going. This is a key sign that what you're going after may not be what you truly want or isn't big enough.

There are a few simple tricks that can help us with discipline or taking action that I will list below.

Activity: The Five-Second Rule

- Whenever you feel there is something you want to do, count backwards from five and then get up and do it. No thinking, no logic. Move your body.

Activity: The Two-Minute Rule

- If you're procrastinating on starting something, try setting a timer for only two minutes long and agree that if you want to stop when you're at the end of it, you can. Oftentimes we will work for much longer than the two minutes.

Activity: Declutter!

- Make a list of as many small tasks around your house as you can, such as cleaning out a junk drawer, doing the dishes, organizing the closet, etc.
- By cleaning out any clutter in your space, you're also cleaning out the clutter in your mind.
- You can focus on the task at hand rather than the many other things you need to get done.

Activity: Show Up

- This applies the same energy as the two-minute rule. It's an exercise about showing up. If you find it difficult to go on a walk, for instance, try putting on your outfit, going outside, and showing up for yourself. Do not decide on a distance. Do not decide on a time. Show up and do your thing. This will build the habit, which is more important than the end result. As the habit forms, you can adjust your goals to go longer, faster, etc.

Start small, build the habit, and adjust.

Confronting Limiting Beliefs

On the path of self-growth, you no doubt will be met with many internal barriers. Among the most impactful will be the limiting beliefs. These are typically beliefs that are ingrained in us from our childhood, how we were raised, our environment, past experiences etc. They operate by coloring our perception, dictating our reactions, and oftentimes leading us away from walking in our truth or opening up to new ideas.

Limiting beliefs may look like:

- "Nothing good will ever happen to me."
- "I need to have a few drinks after work. It's the only thing I can use to reduce my stress."
- "Of course, I forgot my gym sneakers. I'm such an idiot."
- "Success is just something that doesn't happen in my family. We just can't do it."

I'd like to introduce you to cognitive behavioral coaching (CBC), a type of psychological behavioral coaching that specifically deals with unproductive thoughts and feelings that could interfere with your behavior change plans. This field evolved from cognitive behavioral therapy, often used by psychologists and is based in the idea that self-defeating, negative thoughts— "I'll never stick to an exercise program"—can lead to negative emotions (helplessness, anxiety), and will lead to negative behaviors (quitting an exercise program, skipping classes).

As a lifelong learner and coach, I spend quite a bit of time challenging my own beliefs or those of my clients in order to support them to have more productive internal thoughts. Our self-talk, most of the time, are benign thoughts that range from a few words, full sentences, or visualizations of things happening around us or about to happen. Yet self-talk can be counterproductive when it starts to spark feelings of anger, chronic stress, anxiety, doubt, helplessness, or other forms of negative perceptions that then dictate actions that go against our growth.

I myself struggled for over a decade of negative self-talk, constantly feeling I couldn't be enough, thinking I wasn't attractive, and no one would love me. Feeling intense self-hatred, depression, anxiety, and even suicidal thoughts. No longer wanting to be a part of the world due to all the ways I would tell myself life "worked." I created a story and perception of negativity, unknowing how to change or move beyond it. I was stuck.

Once I was fed up with how I was treating myself and dived into the world of the unknown to create change for myself. Previously, my thoughts were typically negative and fear-driven, leading to anxiety. After using these tools and absorbing the insights I learned, I managed to shift my thinking towards more neutral and positive perspectives. This change allowed me to see opportunities and growth most of the time. No longer living in the darkness but allowing myself to see the world for how it actually was. After a while I felt the difference within me. I noticed a shift of my internal environment of how my thoughts went from despairing, unhelpful, hateful to a more reasonable judgment or positive, open-minded etc. This took time but ultimately was what allowed me to step into my power, as it will when you start to reflect on your own internal world.

What I did was start to look at my irrational beliefs and cognitive distortions. We each have our own way of seeing the world, interpreting events and making judgements upon them. Typically, adults have a general understanding of this but operate with the understanding that their perceptions are an accurate representation of reality and may not realize that they are not perceiving the whole picture.

Cognitive distortions refer to irrational thought patterns that can be harmful to a person's well-being. Negative cognitive distortions typically shape how we see events, relationships, and often lead to unproductive views of ourselves or our life.

There are a few common cognitive distortions I'll go over. This will give you an idea of what you can look out for, and every single one of us has them or presents them.

- Jumping to Conclusions (Two types)
  - Mind-reading (imagining we know what others are thinking without evidence)
    - "No one in my family believes I can make a successful business."
  - Fortune-telling (arbitrarily predicting the future and assuming it will turn out bad)
    - "I know if I start my social media with no experience, I'll have so many people who will hate and judge my content."
- All-or-Nothing Thinking (also referred to seeing things as black or white)
  - "Either I do it right or not at all!"
  - "I skipped the gym last week. I might as well forget about the whole exercise plan!"
- Overgeneralizing (seeing one single event as a pattern of defeat or disappointment)
  - "Nothing good ever happens to me,"
  - "Even if I exercise more, I'll never be able to be consistent enough to really lose so much weight."
- Magnification / Minimization (blowing things out of proportion, or shrinking something to make it seem less important)

- o "My stress is so hard for me to deal with that I have to drink in order to contain it."
- o "I've never consistently worked out in my life. Who really cares? I've always felt fine,"
- Labeling (assigning labels to ourselves or others)
  - o "He's such an idiot."
  - o "Of course I missed the gym. I'm an idiot who's horrible at planning."
- Personalization and Blame (blaming yourself for doing something that wasn't completely your fault, or blaming others from something that was your fault)
  - o "All of this is my fault!"
  - o "My parents always fight and yell. That's why I'm always so angry in arguments with others."

There are plenty of irrational beliefs that hold. They come from our families, culture, society, or even past traumas. Some examples of these beliefs could be:

- Self-care is selfish; therefore, it is bad.
- If people disapprove of you, it means you're wrong.
- Always put yourself last and other people first.
- A perfectionist who always feels like a failure as life will never be perfect.

Our beliefs and perceptions create our reality. We only live within the reality we perceive. Two people may see the same event, one may come out of it with a life lesson that inspires them, another may see it as a horrific tragedy which causes them despair. In order to live our most authentic life and get the most out of it, we must shift our perceptions to be growth-based, allowing us to see opportunities as well as ourselves as it is, using discernment.

This does not mean you must be positive about everything. What it means is, if you procrastinated on work, ended up having to catch up, but then missed the gym session you planned, instead of seeing it as a failure, feeling down on yourself, you look in from non-judgmental discernment. You recognize what happened aka procrastination. You then reflect on what you can do better to implement it. It's not about coddling yourself with positive feelings, but rather seeing it for what it is, using your discernment on what you can do better and moving on.

This is a process that takes time. The act is to bring awareness to our internal world so we can begin to transform it. Now that you understand and are aware of how limiting beliefs can affect your life, you can start to reverse the process and challenge them.

Through my coaching experience I've picked up the A-B-C-D-E mnemonic method. It is a framework to help counter unproductive thinking by Albert Eliis.

A - Activating event: Identifying the event that is associated with unproductive thoughts (deciding to skip an exercise session)

B - Belief associated with the event that may have triggered the event ("I haven't worked out all week, so what's the point in going?")

C - Consequences, both physical and emotional (anger, frustration, disappointment)

D - Disputing the negative thinking and reframing the thought with a more productive one ("Missing a week doesn't affect today. Working on myself is still important, and I can go.")

E - Effect, as in the effect of the new positive thoughts that are more productive and helpful ("The past is the past, but every day I can still work towards my goal regardless of how things have been.")

The next framework is the R.E.A.L process.

R - Recognize: Become aware of the negative thought or limiting belief. Acknowledge it without judgment.

E - Examine: What is the origin of this thought? Ask yourself:

- Where did this belief come from?
- Is there any evidence supporting this belief? Or is it something I'm holding on to from past experiences or emotions?

A - Affirm: Create a positive affirmation that counters the negative belief. It should be in present tense alongside coinciding with your own personal truth.

L - Live It Out: Adopt this new affirmation as a part of your daily habits as much as possible. Consistently challenge the negative belief and replace it with a more productive thought.

You could even make your own framework that works for you. It's as simple as recognizing a pattern that is no longer serving you and examining the pattern. "Why do I hold this belief? Does holding onto this belief hurt me or help me? What evidence refutes this belief?" Then, replace this pattern with a more productive thought or habit that does serve you. Think of multiple ways you can replace the pattern and pick one that you believe would work best for you. Then, do your best to integrate the replacement into your daily routine. It's alright if you accidentally repeat the counterproductive pattern. With time, you catch yourself more, adopt positive patterns, and eventually it'll become second nature.

The Growth-Based Mindset

A growth-based mindset is simple in concept. It's the belief that one's skills can be developed through persistent work and effort. Renowned psychologist Dr. Carol Dweck elaborates on this in her study, stating,

"In a growth mindset, people believe that their most basic abilities can be developed through dedication and hard work—brains and talent are just the starting point" (Dweck, 2007). When you're faced with challenges, you know that through effort you can overcome them. A growth mindset sees challenges as an opportunity to grow, rather than a barrier to get stuck on or feel despair from. Utilizing this mindset, you develop resilience through challenges that allow you to keep going. When an idea doesn't serve them or doesn't work out, they are willing to take criticism and keep an open mind to create a new pathway forward, embracing it as a way to develop their skills. Rather than seeing others' success as something to be threatened by, they use their success as a learning opportunity for themselves.

It's always easier learning from the mistakes of others when you can. That's why finding a mentorship, course, book, help, etc. from others who have already achieved what you want to create or become is impactful.

I have a rule, one I learned from the infamous Tai Lopez over ten years ago. You want to surround yourself with three types of people. One is someone who has already achieved what you want to create. The next is someone who is at the same place on the same journey with you, then the third is someone who is on the same path but a bit behind you so you can give back and be a mentor for them. This aligns with numerous studies showcasing the profound impact of mentorship on personal and professional development (Eby et al., 2008).

A fantastic example of a growth mindset is a story told by Tony Robbins, paraphrased here. Tony Robbins has been handing out free food around the holidays for quite some time with his own company. One year, he wanted to get a van and give out as much as he could around neighborhoods in need. He tasked his team to get a van they could stock up and do just that. When Tony returned and asked if they were ready to head out, a member of his team said, "It's not going to happen, Tony. We can't make it happen."

Tony asked, "What do you mean?"

The team replied that every single van in the city had been completely rented out. They called everyone but couldn't find a single van.

Tony said, "Okay, well, I'll find a van," and went out of the office to the main floor (believed to be in New York City). He then stood on the busiest intersection around him, and when the traffic came to a stop at a red light, he would go up to every van he saw and offer to rent out their van for money. Over and over again, they denied him. His own team members were thinking, *what is he doing out there?*

Yet Tony didn't quit, and after a few hours when his team member was telling him to come back, he found someone who said he would help out. Not only would this person help out Tony, but he would do it for free, and he happened to work with people who were in desperate need in the city as well. He told Tony he would drive with him and take him to even more impoverished neighborhoods that desperately needed it.

You can see how such a major setback could have deterred anyone, but with the growth-based mindset, utilizing determination and under-standing that persistence is key, he found himself a van, and it turned out to be an even better situation than what was planned.

I'd like to note, you will hear persistence, aligning yourself with your goal, and using determination over and over again with any motiva-tional speaker or business guru. It is time-tested, because the truth is in the numbers. You *will* find someone that can help you if you spend enough time doing it.

Sure, it might not be the first person you talk to, and it may not be the one hundredth, but number one hundred and one could very well be the person you need to talk to in order to achieve your goal. This works for trying to find a partner, trying to get a car you want, trying to find the right house. In the end, with patience, determination, and effort you will achieve your goal. The only thing that will cause you to stop is yourself.

Another paraphrased quote I'd like to add is from Alex Hormozi, someone I find immense value from. "If your plan didn't work out, that doesn't mean you should change the goal—change the plan."

Here are ways you can foster your own growth-based mindset:

- Mindfulness or Journaling Practices: Engaging in meditation or reflective journaling, you can better see what your attitudes or thoughts are about specific challenges or learning experiences in your life. You can reframe these challenges by asking, "What did I learn from these? How can I improve?" Simply take upon the growth-based mindset and practice from that state of reference.
- Utilize Learning Goals: Create your goals around learning goals, such as getting better at understanding how to lose weight, rather than a performance goal of losing fifty pounds. Learning goals are always easier to accomplish and will get you to your end result.
- Focus on Building Habits, Not Results: Showing up to the gym everyday can be tough, but by showing up, you build the habit and will crush your performance goal. Focusing on losing weight, which takes time, may be discouraging. By focusing on showing up, you do both.
- Embracing Challenges: When you're faced with a challenge, reflect. "How will this better me? What will I gain from this?

What will I learn from this?" Switch this challenge into a learning opportunity.

- Educational Workshops, Reading, YouTube Videos: There is a plethora of information on a growth-based mindset. Simply learn about it to get a better grasp at the mindset and then practice it! Implement it!
  - o Andrew Huberman has a great podcast, which you can find on his YouTube channel.
- Practice the Growth Mindset: As basic as it may seem, a mindset is something to utilize and keep "in mind." Simply try to apply the wisdom of this mindset to your current challenges. It's as easy as remembering what you can learn from this challenge, building resilience by following through, readjusting your plan, or seeking help. Utilize everything you have and by the end of it, you will have learned so much and benefit greatly in every challenge you face.

Stress Is Enhancing Mindset

I want to touch on how we see stress. Chronic physiological stress response in itself can have damaging aspects to our mind, body, and spirit. What I'm talking about is acute stress and our mindset around it.

Stress, when perceived positively or as a challenge, can significantly contribute to fostering a growth-based mindset. This is rooted in the theory of stress mindset, which posits that individuals can hold either a stress-is-enhancing or a stress-is-debilitating mindset. "Stress mindset theory suggests that positive stress beliefs lead to positive, rather than negative, outcomes when engaging with stressors" (Kilby & Sherman, 2016).

In another study following 174 navy seals, they've found "even in this extreme setting, stress-is-enhancing mindsets predict greater persistence through training, faster obstacle course times, and fewer negative evaluations from peers and instructors" (Smith et al., 2020).

There are many studies that show the correlation between having a positive outlook on stress and how it can be beneficial for us. The physiological response serves as a way to pull resources to where we need them to be, rather than cause us disharmony. A faster heart rate could be considered to get the blood pumping, energized and ready for you to act. The narrowing of vision could be utilized for focusing on something specific.

Let me share a story with you. I was in college, my very first public speaking class. I was horrified but knew I had to get past it if I wanted to move forward with my studies. My teacher at the time told us something I've always taken with me. She said to never use the word "nervous" and replace it with "excited." Why?

"Nervous" has a negative connotation when talking about the physiological aspects of stress when public speaking. Your heart goes quicker, you feel narrowed in, your hands start to get a bit sweaty... Now think about being excited. You're about to go on a roller coaster or get a prize. You have a physiological response: your heart goes quicker, you feel narrowed in, your hands start to get a bit sweaty.

You had the exact same physiological response, yet in one way you categorize it as a negative aspect while in the other you view it as something fun. By viewing this stress response in a positive way, not only will it enhance your performance, but it will make it easier to achieve your goals and make it through challenges.

The Transformational Power of Positive Thinking and the Words We Use

Every thought that comes through our mind has the power of changing how we view the world, behaviors we have, or actions we choose. Having a mindset that is based in positivity and gratitude has the ability to create a ripple effect that dramatically changes our lives and the world around us.

I always want to add, this doesn't mean you have to be positive about every single situation. You must expel anger or jealousy from you completely, or you're ruined. What this means is to do your best to come from that state of mind, but life isn't perfect, and neither are any of us. Coming from a positive state of mind is simply helpful.

Being in a positive state of mind can release chemicals such as serotonin and endorphins, which promote well-being, reduce stress, and can enhance focus. This is also why exercise is such a powerful tool to enhance overall well-being, which I'll touch on in Chapter 11.

Not only this, but by seeing challenges or situations in a more positive light (which I genuinely believe is having a growth-based mindset) you will more easily come to solutions to deal with these challenges. Rather than holding anger, jealousy, or other negative emotions which may completely change the actions you choose and create self-destructive behaviors or hurt others around you, which will only bring you further away from your goals. You can come from the mindset of seeing the lessons or positive outcomes within the challenge. Yet, this could also be beneficial as we learn from struggle.

Utilizing negative emotions or thoughts isn't necessarily considered to be a bad thing either. Take, for example, someone who, after a hard breakup, dedicates the next year or their life to self-improvement. In the end, it's all fuel, and what fuel works for you isn't my place to judge or say. David Goggin's fuel is essentially this: talking shit to yourself to motivate yourself.

Positive emotions such as optimism have the ability to influence both our mental well-being and physiology. It helps with an efficient cognitive process, boosting our immune system, gives us greater flexibility to our choices alongside reducing stress or negative effects on the body. Recent epidemiological research has highlighted optimism as a potential predictor of longer life. A study notes, "Higher optimism was associated with longer life span" (Lee et al., 2019). Studies have found a link between higher levels of optimism and a reduced risk of developing chronic diseases associated with aging, as well as a decrease in premature mortality rates.

Moreover, a "positive relationship between optimistic expectancies and cell-mediated immunity (CMI) occurred: Changes in optimism correlated with changes in CMI" (Segerstrom & Sephton, 2010) . This suggests that a positive outlook can have beneficial effects on the immune system's functioning.

These findings show how impactful the growth-based mindset rooted in optimism and positive thinking can have on one's health and longevity, not to mention the spiritual consequences.

Not only is positive thinking important, but so are the words we use. One of the most harmful things we can do is use words that are self-limiting. We discussed earlier the effect of self-limiting beliefs. By reframing the statements and words we use, we can have a dramatic effect on our ability to manifest alongside seeing and creating opportunities for ourselves. It also allows us to take back responsibility for ourselves.

Here are some examples:

Can't

Self-limiting: "I can't complete this task."
Reframed: "I'll find a way to complete this task."

Fail/Failure

Self-limiting: "I failed at my attempt."
Reframed: "I learned from my attempt."

Impossible

Self-limiting: "This goal is impossible."
Reframed: "This goal is challenging but achievable."

Problem

Self-limiting: "I have a problem."
Reframed: "I have an opportunity to improve."

I should

Self-limiting: "I should be better at this."
Reframed: "I can work to improve at this."

I don't know

Self-limiting: "I don't know how to do this."
Reframed: "I can learn how to do this."

Never

Self-limiting: "I'll never get this right."
Reframed: "I'll get this right with practice."

Stuck

Self-limiting: "I'm stuck in this situation."
Reframed: "I'm facing a challenge in this situation."

Too hard

Self-limiting: "This is too hard for me."
Reframed: "This is a challenge for me."

I'm not

Self-limiting: "I'm not good at this."
Reframed: "I'm still learning and improving at this."

Try

Self-limiting: "I'll try to finish it."
Reframed: "I'll finish it."

Hate

Self-limiting: "I hate doing this task."
Reframed: "This task is challenging for me."

I myself practice this to the best of my ability, yet nobody's perfect. All these methods are here to keep in mind and practice. I'm sure in this e-book I have used many of these words. It is all about bringing your awareness to keep it in mind, and not feeling bad or pressuring yourself to always be perfect.

Scarcity vs Abundance Mindset

You've likely heard these terms before, and I'm here to delve into them and why they're crucial for achieving dreams or being useful in everyday life. A scarcity mindset is one of lack, often contemplating what could go wrong, focusing on gaps and shortages. On the other hand, an abundance mindset celebrates what goes right, potentialities, and opportunities present every moment. Like other mindsets, this impacts our behavior, relationships, and overall well-being.

A scarcity mindset isn't merely because you're "negative." In fact, it's a significant part of our reptilian brain. It's part of our early human instincts, as many of our brain's reward systems are. We needed to ensure we had enough food and be on the lookout for dangers threatening ourselves or our tribe. Now, in modern times, without many of these dangers, this mindset manifests differently, focusing on others or ourselves too harshly. Financial anxiety of not wanting to lose what you've acquired when you're in a good position.

Constant worry about what is lacking can lead to poor decision-making. It can put strain on your self-growth or professional development. Many people refuse to go for their dreams because they aren't "ready" or lack the "knowledge" or "guidance." Yet, readiness never truly exists. You will almost never be ready, only as ready as you can be.

With an abundant mindset, you gain enhanced creativity and the ability to see opportunity. You can pull out opportunities from situations easier and feel gratitude for them. Maybe a bad day led you to speak to one specific person that could help you out, maybe it taught you more about yourself and needing to reel back in, maybe you learned what sort of friends you want to be around. Ultimately, with every challenge or situation, you can find both negatives and positives, and the abundant mindset focuses on finding the positives and reflecting on the negatives.

Additionally, this mindset can strain our relationships, thinking competitively against our partners or those around us rather than fostering a collaborative relationship or one of growth. You will build deeper collaborative relationships utilizing an abundant mindset. No one makes it to the top without the help of others. Well...you can, but where's the fun in that? Why not help raise those around you as you rise? Why not build yourself a beautiful community of like-minded individuals looking to achieve similar things as you? In business, I've learned, the best way to make money is to help others make it first. We are all in this together.

An abundance mindset has also been found to help with overall well-being, life satisfaction, and being happier. "Experiencing gratitude, thankfulness, and appreciation tends to foster positive feelings, which in turn, contribute to one's overall sense of wellbeing. Therefore, gratitude appears to be one component, among many components, that contributes to an individual's wellbeing." (Sansone and Sansone, 2010).

There are many reasons why you may want to practice an abundant mindset, yet how do we switch from scarcity to abundant?

You can utilize many tools:

- **Meditation or Mindfulness:** Cultivate an awareness of where your thoughts are at and shift them towards an abundance mindset.
- **Gratitude Practice:** You can do this upon waking or anytime during your day. Pause and think of three things you have deep gratitude for. Focus on what you have in abundance rather than in lack. It can be as simple as the water we drink, relationships, family, the sun, life, or something that hits deeper for you.
- **Affirmations and Visualizations:** Remind yourself that we are always abundant. Oftentimes we have the resources to get what we want. It's about becoming resourceful, utilizing what we have to achieve our goals rather than what we don't. Visualize yourself in a state of abundance, having everything you want to attract to you.

Ultimately, abundance is all around us. What stops us from receiving is our inability to accept abundance. It's about tapping back into that abundance and seeing the opportunities that are constantly arriving around us.

Switching our mind from a scarcity to abundant mindset can be a challenge, but our job is to walk the path. We must hold awareness, catch ourselves when we can, and implement the mindset that works for us. By doing this, you literally are living the life you wanted to have.

Dive into Law of Attraction

The law of attraction is rooted in the belief that a vibrational frequency being emitted from our thoughts and emotions will attract that same frequency. The primary operating principle is that "like attracts like." Positive thoughts are believed to attract positive circumstances while negative thoughts will attract undesirable outcomes.

How this works is that by aligning our mental state and emotions with the outcome we desire, we then set the stage for the universe to respond in kind. We are pulling towards us the exact outcome that our frequency is sending out to the universe. Rather than life happening to us, we now gain an understanding that gives us power to create our life by design. We are an active part in creating our reality.

Regardless of if you believe this or not, we are always manifesting the life we desire or the life we do not. Every action, choice, thought is used to create our reality around us. Whether you take this principle in its metaphysical form as a true energetic law, or as we discussed the Reticular Activating System earlier, being in that mindset allows you to see opportunity, it will be a principle to consider.

I spoke on utilizing your vibrational frequency. What is that? Every thought, emotion, and being emits a specific type of energy that gives off its own vibrational frequency. You can imagine this like tuning into a radio station. Depending on what you're tuned into, it is what you attract and how you perceive the world around us. On a deeper look into people who "tune" into gratitude, positivity, or other high vibrational emotions, we can find it has positive effects on our physiology.

The universe itself has endless possibilities and only gives us what we tune into. I also tend to think it sends us challenges to move us in certain directions, to keep us in line with whatever our mission may be here, but that's for another book.

When we have positive thoughts and emotions, we emit a higher vibrational frequency, attracting circumstances and energies that resonate with this positivity. Conversely, when we dwell in negative thoughts and emotions, we lower our vibrational frequency, attracting less desirable conditions and energies into our lives.

Manifestation uses this understanding of the LoA by aligning your emotions and thoughts to then attract opportunities or circumstances that you can act upon. You can do this by meditating, then focusing deeply on what your desired outcome is and pairing it with a strong emotion (joy, gratitude, excitement, love, compassion). When you focus on your outcome, you need to visualize it as if it has already happened.

The universe is quite literal. For instance, if you're focused on how badly you "want," say, a pair of shoes, you will then manifest exactly that and get it immediately, because here you are wanting a pair of shoes! To manifest something, you must only think of it in terms of experiencing it as if it has already happened. You visualize yourself in your new car, driving it, feeling excited and happy your success led to this, feeling the wind in your hair, hearing the motor go. As detailed as you can go, the better it'll manifest.

Also to note, how it manifests is not up to you. You do not get to decide how this comes to you, only have faith that it will.

Some of the best methods to make this happen is through daily meditation, visualizations, affirmations, and focusing on gratitude or other higher vibrational emotions. Really feel yourself and the emotion you choose while visualizing your desired outcome. Truly feel gratitude, love, etc. The more you practice, the better you will get at this.

A common misconception that people have is that merely having positive thoughts surrounding an outcome will allow it to manifest. This is completely untrue. Without pairing it with action, almost nothing will come of it. You can manifest yourself on a private island, but now imagine all the different events that will need to happen to get you there, likely fifty or more than a hundred. You aren't a magician creating things out of thin air. If you want a private island, the universe will test you with opportunities, challenges and events that will get you there. Depending on how quickly you take action, see the opportunities, and become aligned to that outcome, will determine if you manifest that desire or not.

You may manifest the outcome, but without seeing the opportunities, you may miss being able to truly have it.

Another aspect is relationships or love. You may want to create a situation where you have a perfect partner, and in order to get that...you again have to be aligned with that, alongside that person being aligned in the same way. Like attracts like. If you aren't a perfect partner, it's unlikely you will find a perfect partner. If you want a unicorn, you must become a unicorn. We will always end up around others who are aligned with us for better or worse.

Manifestation is essentially a test process to see if you're ready. The universe goes "Ooooh, I see what you're trying to get now. Let me send you a few connections, job opportunities, challenges to get through." You then have to take action and move forward on what appears. Maybe you're in the exact same coffee shop as someone who can drastically change your life towards where you want to go. You overhear something and feel like you should go talk to them...but you decide not to out of fear or feeling rushed to go somewhere. Well, you won't make the connection.

If you want to be an athlete, you have to take action like an athlete.

Here are a few daily practices you can utilize:

Morning Meditation:

- ◎ Settle into a comfortable position and close your eyes.
- ◎ Clearly picture what you wish to achieve. Imagine it in vivid detail—what it looks like, how it feels to have achieved it, and the positive changes it brings to your life.
- ◎ Step into your visualization. Feel the emotions—joy, gratitude, excitement—as if your success is real right now.
- ◎ Let these positive emotions fill you, reinforcing the sense of achievement and fulfillment.

Target Cycling:

- ◎ Write down a list of ten things you want to manifest, in order from easiest to achieve and hardest to achieve.
- ◎ Create a slideshow with each slide being a corresponding image of one of the things you want to manifest. It can be anything that visualizes what you're manifesting. Do this for all ten slides.
- ◎ Every day, view and cycle through this slideshow. Once you can go through each thing you want to manifest without using the software, you will then meditate on each of these.

- Meditate, going through each of your ten manifestations repeatedly and do this for a minimum of ten to twenty minutes.
- Note that this will require you to get adept enough in meditation to be able to fully relax and get into a deeper state of consciousness. The more consistent you are with your practice, the quicker you'll learn.

Symbolic Burning

- Write down each of your manifestations on a piece of paper.
- Set your intention to the universe that these will be manifested, and you will take action.
- Burn the paper.
- You can also do this for aspects that no longer serve you and release them to the universe. What matters is purely your intention behind it.

Manifest Symbol

- Similar to the target cycling, you will create a symbol for the desire you are manifesting. To make it simple, you could make it a letter J for "job," or R for "relationship," etc.
- Then underneath the symbol, you will write exactly what you want to manifest, in terms of a job, it could be: "$75,000/year," "working with disabled individuals," "I work outside," etc. Be as detailed and literal as possible.
- Now you will enter into your meditation and focus on this symbol. Do your best to only visualize it with a strong positive emotion and view it as if it's already happened and feel that truth deeply within your body and soul.

Fake It Until You Make It: Act as if you already manifested your desires. This will align you to the frequency of your outcome. It'll prepare you for any choices that may come, and ultimately, the more we intentionally act and come from this space, the closer you will not only come to achieving it but actually become it.

A side note for meditating, which I'll detail more in Chapter 10 discussing energy work is to get yourself primed up and relaxed before you get into trying to manifest. This way, you're aligned internally before you begin.

You can do this by focusing on anything that brings love, joy, compassion, or gratitude into your life. Your family, friends, job or even your progress on your journey. Anything! After doing and feeling that for five to ten minutes or when you feel ready, change your focus to your cycling practice, visualization of it happening, or the symbol you created.

Utilizing a mind movie as I mentioned in Chapter 7 is also great for this type of work. Always believe in yourself. Know that you will manifest it with intentional action and stay focused on your desired outcome. A book that greatly helped me was Joe Dispenza's *Becoming Supernatural*, alongside his *You Are the Placebo*. If you want more in-depth, science-based books, these are my go-tos for you.

By making small daily practices more common, you will more easily achieve your desired outcome. These shouldn't completely overhaul your current lifestyle and become cumbersome. Rather, find what works best for you, and over time, these small adjustments will culminate in more positivity, abundance, and ultimately get closer to a fulfilling life that is designed by you!

An interpretation in the Book of John I felt compelled to share, I found through Gregg Braden. You may know "Ask and you will receive," but a different decoding of the text says,

"Ask without hidden motive and be surrounded by your answer. Be enveloped by what you desire that your gladness be full."

Its important to note, "hidden motive" may refer to egotistical desires, money, fame etc. Your intention matters deeply.

Feel as if your prayer is answered, your body is healed. Have no judgment on what the outcome will be. Have gratitude for it.

I highly recommend watching his YouTube video called, "Gregg Braden—Our Most Cherished Ancient Spiritual Technology Explained."

Personal Responsibility

Before I close out this chapter, I want to talk about what I would say is one of the largest factors of success, which is taking personal responsibility for your life and how it turns out. One of the best things you can do is adopt your own responsibility. By doing this, we recognize and accept our own personal power and control over our actions, decisions, reactions, and ultimately our life trajectory.

This involves understanding that the quality of our life is a direct reflection of our thought patterns, behaviors, and attitudes to identify any limiting or self-sabotaging beliefs. Cultivating this self-awareness allows for a deeper understanding of ourselves and the world around us.

With this, we need to overcome a victim mentality, a state in which we blame or feel helpless from the external factors that happen around us. Being in this mentality is a surefire way to hinder your personal growth. We must allow the external circumstances to happen, reflect upon them and use a growth-based mindset or reflection on what we could have done better or differently to then guide our future decisions.

Every time we blame something outside of us, we acknowledge to ourselves, peers, and even the universe at large that we are giving away our power. That we do not have control over our life or circumstances that happen. When we do that, we then enter into a state of helplessness, which will cause us to no longer see the decisions that need to be made. We no longer see the growth in the challenges.

We can take back personal responsibility by having an honest conversation with ourselves about whatever the current situation is, why you have not gone towards your dreams yet or feel stuck. Truly innerstanding without judgment on what has gone awry and how you can start piecing it back together to be aligned towards a life you want to live.

Accountability practices, such as reflective journaling or seeking constructive feedback, can provide valuable insights and foster a growth-oriented mindset. One of the best practices we can use is simply coming from the mindset that we are one hundred percent responsible for everything that happens to us. That every argument, bad habit, accident, short-coming, etc. is completely your responsibility.

Now, I know that if a plane fell out of the sky and somehow landed on you, how could you be responsible? What we're doing when we come from this mindset is say that you could not have gone outside that day, you could have stayed longer at a coffee shop, you could have made choices that didn't cause that plane to land on you.

We can take this stance, for example, in a relationship. Say you had a horrible fight with your significant other. If we say okay, we are completely responsible for this, we start to think, *how could I have said something to communicate better? Maybe my body language was incredibly off putting. Maybe what I did was really uncool.*

What it does is causes us to reflect on what other actions we could have taken to get to our perceived wanted outcome. No, not everything has to be necessarily your responsibility, but by using it as a mindset, you can start to see many ways you can improve.

Conclusion

Our mental stance holds the keys to the quality of life we lead. The growth mindset, Law of Attraction, and personal responsibility are not just concepts, but powerful tools for sculpting our reality. They beckon us to step beyond passive existence into a realm of active creation, where each thought and action is a deliberate stride towards our desired outcomes. The essence of this section is simple yet profound— by nurturing a positive mindset and taking charge of our thoughts, we set a sturdy foundation for a fulfilling life journey. This isn't only a call to understand these principles, but an invitation to embody them, to weave them into the fabric of our daily lives and in doing so, unlock a world brimming with possibilities.

Author's Note: My goal is to serve others when they feel called to do so. If you're looking to go deeper on these topics, I invite you to give me a call to see if you'd like to work one on one with yours truly.

*Mightywellness.*us/schedule

One does not become enlightened by imagining figures of light, but by making the darkness conscious.

- CARL JUNG

09

Shadow Work

Shadow work is another major component to the work we do in order to create our most aligned reality. Similar to encountering limiting beliefs while facing challenges We will also be faced with dealing with our shadow. Unexplored shadows serve as an opportunity to provide insight into ourselves on a deeper level. Shadow work itself is a practice rooted in unveiling the hidden aspects of our psyche, aspects that take place in the subconscious realm of our minds yet have a massive impact on our conscious interactions.

This concept originated in analytical psychology, introduced by the Swiss psychiatrist Carl Jung. The shadow can be defined as the unknown dark side of our personality, where both undeveloped and unexpressed traits reside alongside aspects of ourselves that we deem less desirable. The shadow itself is a mirror into our fears, insecurities, suppressed emotions and inherent wisdom.

Understanding our shadow takes us on its own journey towards finding our most authentic and whole self. It allows us to shine light on the dark corners of our inner world to foster self-acceptance, growth, and healing. The significance of this can have major impacts on our perception, relationships, and our collective consciousness.

It's important to note that there may be traumatic events or emotions that are incredibly difficult to deal with, and it may be best to explore those with a professional to help guide you. Shadow work is incredibly powerful, but unless we meet it with the right tools and a safe environment, we can re-trigger emotional responses or traumas in our lives that had a major impact on us.

ACTIVITY: Reflection Exercise – Identifying Your Initial Reaction to Shadow Work

As we step into the realm of shadow work, let's gauge our initial thoughts and reactions.

- What initial emotions or thoughts arrive when considering diving into your own personal shadow?
- How do you feel about uncovering aspects of yourself that have been in the dark?
- Are there any feelings of fear? What excites you about this journey?

Jot down your initial thoughts and reflections into a journal. This serves as a point of reference as we go deeper into the shadow.

The Importance of Shadow Work

Shadow work isn't just about uncovering your own shadow; it's to take those insights and integrate them to foster a deeper innerstanding of the self, to step into a realm of self-discovery to benefit our own growth, enhance our relationships, and heal past wounds we may have.

Let's dive into some of the impactful dimensions of shadow work.

Personal Growth and Awareness:

Engaging with shadow work allows you to have a deeper insight into yourself, giving you a well-rounded self-awareness, which is a cornerstone to personal growth. You will uncover hidden aspects of your psyche and gain insights into your behaviors, reactions, and tendencies. This awareness will allow you to break past limiting beliefs and patterns in order to pave a way towards your ultimate vision.

Enhancing Relationships and Communication

As you become more familiar with your inner workings and start to integrate wisdom you've gained from the shadow, you will undoubtedly see the effects in your own personal life and within the relationships of others you communicate towards. The shadow allows for a compassionate understanding of your reactions and interactions, which in turn allows for more authentic communication. By understanding your own personal triggers, you will cultivate healthier, more fulfilling relationships.

Healing Past Wounds and Fostering Self-Compassion

Oftentimes the shadow holds past wounds, suppressed emotions, and unresolved conflicts. Engaging with these lesser-known aspects of the self gives you an opportunity to meet them with compassionate understanding to facilitate healing. This is a journey of embracing our vulnerabilities, to acknowledge them for what they are and use the insights to fuel the most authentic version of ourselves.

ACTIVITY: Journaling Prompt - Noticing Patterns in Personal or Interpersonal Dynamics

Grab a journal and take some quiet time to reflect on the following:

1. Identify any recurring themes or patterns in your reactions, especially during challenging or triggering situations.
2. How do these patterns manifest in your relationships and communication?

3. How might understanding your shadow self-contribute to transforming these patterns and enhancing your relationships?

Through these reflections, you begin to sketch the outlines of your shadow, forming the initial steps into a journey of deeper self-exploration and transformation.

Uncovering Your Shadows

When we dive into uncovering our shadow, it takes us on a path that is both introspective and illuminating. It is also important to create a safe space when exploring this realm with compassion, love, and without judgment to yourself or others. At times exploring the shadow can be a difficult process and without the proper mindset going in, it could re-trigger you to whatever you may be focusing on. This will require a unique blend of self-reflection and mindful observation.

Self-reflection and Mindfulness Practices:

To begin with uncovering the shadow, we must have a willingness to look inward. You can use a variety of reflection and mindful practices in order to see into the lesser-known parts of our psyche. By cultivating mindfulness, you will create a space of non-judgmental awareness and compassion, allowing yourself to see these parts, yet be disconnected from them. View them as something you are observing rather than something that is currently happening.

Recognizing Triggers and Personal Reactions

A significant portion of shadow work revolves around recognizing your own personal triggers and how you react to certain situations. This could be everything from how a boss or family member talks to you, which causes a negative reaction or triggers an emotional response within, to situations that may cause you to feel less than or down on yourself, such as feeling bad for not keeping a promise. Again, it's important to stay open and compassionate as through this work we will start to see patterns that can be hard to acknowledge or admit. Yet if we make it through, we can begin to change towards behaviors and patterns that serve us to our highest self.

ACTIVITY: Mindfulness Meditation - Observing Emotional Responses and Triggers

For this activity, allocate a quiet time and space where you can sit comfortably without interruptions.

- Begin by taking a few deep breaths, settling into a state of relaxation and openness.
- As you continue to breathe gently, bring your attention to your inner world. Notice any emotions or thoughts that arise without attempting to change or judge them.
- Now, reflect on a recent situation that triggered an emotional reaction in you. Replay the scenario in your mind, observing the emotions that surface.
- As you observe, remain detached, viewing your emotional responses as a compassionate witness.
- Jot down your observations in a journal, noting any patterns, recurrent emotions, or insights that emerge regarding your triggers.
- Reflect on how these insights provide a glimpse into your shadow self, and how they can serve as steppingstones for deeper exploration.

Navigating through Shadows with Compassion and Gratitude

As we move through experiencing our shadow, we will be met with rather tender aspects of our being. These could evoke a wide array of emotions; hence, it is important to come into this work with a compassionate, loving, and grateful heart. This will pave the way towards a nurturing exploration of our shadow.

We can create a safe environment for this work in a variety of ways.

- Preparing mentally for the work and setting a clear intention for the session.
- Reminding ourselves of the purpose and growth that will come of this.
- Cultivating mindfulness and staying present with whatever arises without judgment. Being gentle with ourselves as shadow work can be quite taxing.
- it's important to come in with compassion and self-forgiveness.

If what you're exploring is deep or traumatic areas, consider working with a professional therapist or coach who is experienced in these matters and can provide a safe container for exploration. Alongside this, engaging with communities that are also doing similar self-work can be powerful as you share your experiences with each other. Make sure to consider boundaries of what is safe to explore, or what might need professional support.

Always celebrate the wins of what you've learned and document your progress in a journal or any format that works for you.

Now let's explore some practices that are beneficial for shadow work.

ACTIVITY: Guided Self-Compassion Meditation and Forgiveness Exercise

Self-Compassion Meditation:

- Find a quiet, comfortable space where you won't be disturbed.
- Close your eyes and take a few deep breaths to center yourself.
- Visualize your heart center glowing with a warm, gentle light.
- As you breathe in, imagine this light expanding, enveloping your entire being with compassion and love.
- Breathe out any self-judgment, criticism, or negative emotions, visualizing them dissolving into the light.
- Repeat this process for a few minutes, immersing yourself in the energy of self-compassion and love.

Heart-Brain Coherence Meditation:

This one I learned from Greg Braden, who is a supporter of Heart Math Institute, the one that specifically made this meditation and has a lovely amount of research on the science of our heart and emotions, which is incredibly impactful. I strongly recommend this specifically when dealing with emotional situations.

- Find a comfortable location, either sitting or lying down, that is quiet and allows you to focus.
- Take deep breaths. Seven seconds in, hold for a few seconds, seven seconds out. Do this for five to ten minutes. (You will continue this throughout the whole meditation. The five to ten minutes is to get you into a relaxed state before beginning.)
- Once you feel relaxed, focus on creating a connection between your heart and your brain. You can visualize a simple line that connects the two.

- If focusing on your heart is difficult, try putting a hand over it to build that connection.
- Now as you make that connection, think about something that brings you great joy, love, or gratitude (family, a situation, recent accomplishment, nature, etc.)
- Feel that emotion wash over your body and sit in it for at least five minutes, but for as long as you would like.

This meditation will prime you for coming from a heart-centered space. It also has amazing mental and physiological benefits that I will talk about in the next chapter. (You can find many guided meditations of this on YouTube)

Forgiveness Exercise:

- On a piece of paper, jot down any resentments, grievances, or judgments you hold towards yourself or others.
- Reflect on each item, and as you do, visualize yourself extending forgiveness, releasing the burden associated with these emotions.
- If comfortable, you may say out loud or silently, "I forgive myself for..." or "I forgive [name] for..." as you work through each item.
- Conclude by expressing gratitude for the insights and growth opportunities these experiences have provided.

These practices will help nurture a forgiving attitude towards yourself and others, alongside cultivating self-compassion. They help build the foundation that is needed to create a safe internal environment for anything you may encounter within your shadow.

Integrating Shadow Lessons into Daily Life

Shadow work itself is a powerful tool when we utilize it for its transformative potential, taking the insights, wisdom, and understandings that we gain from it and then creating an action plan, choice, or attitude that we can integrate into our daily lives. This section will give you a glance on how to turn insight into action to support your personal growth.

An example could be that every time say, someone asks you about finding a job or a project you're working on, you tend to not want to talk about it, get frustrated at them for asking, think negative thoughts towards them, or feel embarrassed about it. You can ask why you are feeling this way. It could be because you aren't putting in the work, you've been procrastinating, not choosing actions that benefit you towards that goal or feel fear about doing it, etc.

The insight we gain is that one, we don't need to react negatively and can be truthful about what's going on. Second, we can acknowledge what's been going wrong with the situation which causes those emotions and then choose differently. There are many ways we can gain insight from these reactions we see, and any amount of wisdom that can be integrated is an absolute win.

Transforming Insights into Actionable Changes

- Conscious Awareness: When we carry the awareness cultivated during shadow work in our daily interactions and responses, we can then identify old patterns that no longer serve us and choose to respond from a newfound place of understanding.
- Practical Application: Identify different areas in your life where the insights gained could be applied. Whether that's

improving communication, fostering healthier relationships, changing self-sabotaging behaviors, or keeping promises to yourself. Pinpoint what is currently happening and what steps can be taken to create change. Bring in conscious awareness to catch yourself and then do your best to implement your plan.

Building a Supportive Environment for Continuous Growth

- Continued Learning: Implement the growth-based mindset and with whatever insights you gained, find some books, courses, mentors, or workshops that can help you learn the skills you need to move beyond the challenges.
  - For example, *The Zen of Listening* by Rebecca Shaffir was incredibly helpful for me to learn how to communicate better. I always could communicate but had many challenges in my relationship or with others by being too excited or wanting to always share (that Leo energy), which stemmed from being antisocial, shut off and scared of speaking as a child. We can *always* learn skills to improve areas. We are *never* just "born that way."
- Practical Application: Implement any mindful practices that help keep that conscious awareness alive. Through meditation, journaling, and mindfulness, we can maintain that inner connection with ourselves and also track our patterns and progress as we move through these areas of growth.

ACTIVITY: Creating a Reflection Routine

- **Time Allocation:** Create either a daily or weekly moment in which you can reflect on the day, either in the morning to set the tone for the day, or the evening to process the day's event.
- **Journaling:** Keep a journal to track the thoughts, growth, and patterns you find important that you noticed and include notes on how you would like to deal with it next time.
- **Mindful Observation:** Throughout the day, keep a mindful awareness of your reactions, behaviors, and thoughts or potential triggers and how you respond to them.

Reflective Questions:

- o   What did I learn about myself today?
- o   How did I respond to challenges?
- o   What can I do differently?

ACTIVITY: Establishing Support

- Reach out to friends, family, or colleagues who are interested in personal growth, shadow work, or self-improvement that you can share your insights with and discuss your progress.
- Join a group whether online or in person, with members that share the same journey that you are going on.

All these activities are to help you transform these insights into action and gain a deeper level of innerstanding about your shadows, propelling you towards a journey of self-exploration and going hand in hand with our mindset Chapter 8.

My Personal Reflection on Shadow Work

Shadow work, along with uncovering limiting beliefs, has to be one of the most powerful tools I've used in my own personal journey. I already found it quite easy before I found out what shadow work was, as I was always focused on the negative aspects of my being. I was constantly in a state where I would shut myself down in conversation because what I had to say wouldn't be "important" or "valuable," or wanting to disrespect who I was talking to. I would get down on myself for not being able to be consistent with my gym schedule, keeping promises to myself. The most pain I felt was that all these traits were exactly the opposite from the person I knew I was, and the emotions I felt were deep knowing what I could become and what was inside of me.

The first practice I ever did was reflecting on past experiences I deemed negative and pulling out the insight and wisdom from those to then implement in my life—a main component of shadow work. I was practicing all along without ever really knowing it. As I developed a taste for reading Carl Jung and diving deeper into this area, I gained insight into what shadow work was and how I could use it to be beneficial.

The insights I gained were that I was beautiful wherever I was in my journey, that what I had to say was valuable, and if it wasn't, frankly, who gives a shit. I deserve to be able to express my authentic self. I deserve to hold myself in high regard, regardless of how much work I've put in the past. My job isn't to time travel into the past and fix all my mistakes—the mistakes *are* my journey, and the insights I gained are the unique wisdom that take me to the next level.

What I gained from shadow work, and this work in general, was the gift of awareness. I was no longer a walking pity party, upset at myself and others, having no idea what was happening like a sad robotic. I was able to actively see what was happening, find compassion for myself, a deep love for who I was, and then move forward in the direction I chose to go in. I became and realized my full potential as a Divine Creator of this reality.

These small, daily changes had a massive ripple effect throughout every aspect of my life. I will also repeat myself, again and again, this all takes *time*. You will *not* be perfect and immediately become your highest self. You *will* make mistakes. You will face many challenges. You cannot expect to do everything right, fully realized, on an exact schedule where it all turns out exactly as it should. What you're aiming for is one percent daily improvement, which is a three hundred sixty-five percent return every year. More so, the faster you execute on your ideas, the more consistent you are. Your one percent can be two percent daily, three percent daily, and work yourself up.

"

If you want to find the secrets of the universe, think in terms of energy, frequency, and vibration.

- NIKOLA TESLA

10

Energy Work - Balancing and Nurturing Your Inner Self

Ah, yes, the type of work that set it all off for me. Learning about energy work and the different practices within was the largest catalyst when I was younger to go on a journey of self-exploration. Energy work can have many connotations, and we'll be going over both metaphysical and practical applications.

It in itself is a way of viewing the world and also understanding the energetic nature of it and of ourselves, emotions, physical body, and ways that we can transmute it to work for us. Learning how to reach heart-centered states of being, clearing our energy, or keeping a check on the type of energy we receive from others. Everything in life is an energetic practice, the way we speak to and receive from others.

Everything has its own energetic signature, emotions, nature, our bodies. The earth itself has its own frequency, known as the Schumann resonance. Humans are fantastic receivers and givers of energy, as if we have an antenna that can pick it up and send it out. When we enter a room, you can intuitively sense the "energy" of that room. Or when we see someone who is in pain, hurt, struggling, happy, joyous we can also sense that. In part, this is also being able to perceive the physical elements and body language alongside the subtle energies those create.

We also have our own energetic frequency that extends around three feet from our bodies. This frequency is generated from our hearts and can be detected by advanced technology (SQUID-based magnetometers are one such way). The energy we let out is directly correlated to our inner world. Whether that's anxiety, fear, or love and gratitude. These emotions also leave lasting physiological markers.

When I say energy, I'm specifically speaking on the electromagnetic signatures we give off. As we learn to recognize our own subtle energy and that of others, we can better attune ourselves to a frequency that is most beneficial for our self-growth. This of course has an impact on our environment, relationships, and many other areas of life. As we go deeper into this chapter, we will discuss how to utilize our energy, ground ourselves, protect it, and have a better understanding of how we can use it to benefit our alignment.

Benefits of Meditation

Two of the most potent tools you can learn and implement into your daily routine are meditation and breathwork. Meditation itself is a tool you can use to change your brainwaves to enter into altered states of consciousness. This can be used to relax yourself, dive into your subconscious, have out-of-body experiences, reprogram your thought patterns, and many other practical advantages I'll list below.

The physiological benefits of meditation are numerous and well documented. Through consistent practice, individuals can see improvement in many areas, from cognitive functioning to stress reduction and overall health and well-being.

Stress Reduction:

- Meditation, particularly mindfulness-based cognitive therapy (MBCT), has been found to lessen negative thoughts or

- unhelpful emotional reactions in times of stress (American Psychological Association, 2019).
- A systematic review and meta-analysis highlighted the effectiveness of mindfulness-based programs in reducing psychological distress among medical students (da Silva et al., 2023).
- Mindfulness-based stress reduction (MBSR) has been compared favorably to standard treatments like escitalopram for anxiety disorders (Hoge et al., 2023).
- Controlled breathwork, akin to meditation practices, was shown to improve mood and reduce anxiety in a study (Balban et al., 2023).

Cognitive Functioning:

- Mindfulness meditation has demonstrated potential to offset normal age-related cognitive decline and enhance cognitive function (*The impact of meditation on cognitive function* 2020).
- Just ten minutes a day of mindfulness meditation improves concentration and working memory (Malinowski Reader in Cognitive Neuroscience, 2018).
- Mindfulness-based stress reduction (MBSR) may improve attention, executive function, or working memory in middle-aged or older adults, as well as in patients with mild cognitive impairment (MCI) (Mckeehan, 2020).
- In MCI, mindfulness has shown to improve cognition, quality of life, and well-being (Ziedman, 2022).

Focus:

- A short mindfulness meditation session can improve motor control and selective attention, with benefits noted in both novices and experienced meditators (Dolan, 2023).

- Mindfulness meditation specifically enhanced the intentional maintenance of a specific motor coordination pattern, indicating an improvement in motor control skills even after a fifteen-minute session (Dolan, 2023).

Emotional Regulation:

- Mindfulness meditation may reduce interference from emotional distractions, particularly positive ones, in various perceptual load conditions, showing improved attentional control and reduced emotional distraction compared to non-meditators (Dolan, 2023).
- The practice of mindfulness meditation can improve the ability to manage distractions and process emotions more efficiently, reducing the need to seek satisfaction from external pleasurable distractions (Dolan, 2023).

Mindfulness Meditation and Mood Disorders:

- Mindfulness-based interventions for anxiety can have a moderate effect size, though some reviews and meta-analyses have pointed out methodological deficits in meditation studies (Hoge et al., 2013).
- Another study examined the effects of mindfulness meditation compared to breathwork on mood, anxiety, and other physiological measures, finding enhancements in mood and reductions in anxiety among participants (Balban et al., 2023).

Managing Stress Through Spirituality:

- In the wake of heightened post-COVID anxiety, turning to spiritual practices has been shown to improve mental well-being and physical health (Woodcock, 2023).

- Spirituality can be a potent means for individuals to manage stress, with paths such as developing an inner life, embracing a calling, and creating a community being particularly beneficial (Woodcock, 2023).

Exploration of Inner Life:

- Individuals with rich inner lives are more in touch with their true selves, encompassing their hopes, dreams, thoughts, emotions, instincts, and intuition. Spiritual practices like meditation and prayer can provide a sense of value and connection to a higher being or larger life scheme, aiding in managing anxiety and establishing greater well-being (Woodcock, 2023).

Comparative Effectiveness of Mindfulness:

- A review of over two hundred studies on mindfulness among healthy individuals found that mindfulness-based therapy was especially effective for reducing stress, anxiety, and depression, and could also help treat people with specific problems including depression, pain, smoking, and addiction (*Mindfulness meditation: A research-proven way to reduce stress* 2019).
- Some research suggests that meditation and mindfulness may be as effective as medication for treating certain mental health issues, offering a non-pharmacological approach to managing these conditions (Marusak, 2023).

Meditation Tips

Before we begin listing out techniques, I'm going to cover the major tips and pitfalls I've come across and helped others with regarding meditation. Meditation, like anything, is a practice that takes time to master. Some can learn it quickly, while others may take more time. The faster we execute on the practice, the quicker we become adjusted to meditating.

Meditation can be used for a variety of reasons as we listed above. What it comes down to is being able to relax within your body, focus with a set intention, and explore your inner self. How you choose to meditate is truly up to you and for whatever intention you choose.

As we become more adept at meditating, we can start to shift into altered states of consciousness, utilize the "field" of energy all around us to manifest and change our brainwaves for specific results, such as incredibly quick learning or info retention utilizing gamma brain waves (which only touches the surface of this). If you want more detailed information, I found Joe Dispenza to be an indispensable resource on this topic, and his book *Becoming Supernatural* is a banger.

Tip 1: Monkey Brain

Often when you first begin meditating, you may imagine that goal is to quiet the mind, and the truth is, sometimes it is depending on the meditation. As you begin you may notice the mind is incredibly active, with how your day is going, anxieties, tasks you need to get done, or even thoughts thinking about how silly this may be or how difficult it is to quiet your mind or how bad you are at meditating. This mind chatter is known as "monkey brain."

Solution: Meditation is like building a muscle. You will have to manually refocus your attention on your breathing, your chest rising and falling or any other physical sensation or sensory information coming in. Also, monkey brain isn't bad. Oftentimes taking a backseat and watching the thoughts without judgment will teach you a lot about what's going on with yourself.

When you catch your mind wandering, refocus on your breathing.

Tip 2: Frustration

When we begin a new skill, it can be uncomfortable or strange. When our mind wanders, doesn't feel relaxed, or feel like it has accomplished anything, frustration and many other negative emotions can start to emerge.

Solution: Have no expectations for how the session will go. Similar to working out, it may take time to see the results. As you continue to practice, it becomes easier and eventually starts to connect with you. Come into the practice with your intention alongside knowing this is a practice that takes time to get used to. With this in mind, you can never "fail" a meditation session.

Tip 3: Distractions

It's common to be distracted from external noises or interruptions during meditation, which can disrupt your session.

Solution: Create a conducive environment for meditation. This may be done through finding a quiet environment, using headphones with white noise or that are noise canceling. Alongside this, as we become distracted, refocus on your breathing or audio that you have on.

Tip 4: Physical Discomfort

Sitting for a long period of time can lead to discomfort.

Solution: Choose a comfortable position that you can maintain throughout the entire session. You can try sitting, lying down, or even a walking meditation. Use cushions or props as needed. Gently adjust your position and refocus on the meditation, breath, etc.

I almost never meditate sitting. I prefer to lie down on my back with either no pillow or a thin one. What works best for you is what is always recommended. Try out different methods and create your own space.

Tip 5: Restlessness

You may get frustrated from an itch, discomfort, or simply not being in the mood.

Solution: Having to scratch an itch, move because of discomfort, or finding it difficult to get into the "mood" to meditate, does not mean it's a bad session. Adjust yourself, scratch that itch and refocus on your breathing. I often thought this was true and realized it was even more distracting trying to not "move" in fear of ruining the meditation, rather than just taking action and letting it go, to get back into it.

Tip 6: Sleepiness

Sometimes you may experience yourself falling asleep or dozing off.

Solution: Find a time in your day where you are most alert. I quite enjoy meditating in the morning or night because in that zone between awake and asleep, we are most suggestible, making it easier to get into a trance state. I chose to embrace sleepiness, and it was a large part of my dream practices when I was younger. Again, if this is a problem, you can do it in a state more awake. If not, try embracing the sleep.

Tip 7: Overwhelmed by Emotions

After getting deeper into meditations over the years, I started to feel deep emotions of joy, happiness, sometimes even realizations or epiphanies of current situations. I almost always start to cry from this. You may feel a wide range of emotions being released.

Solution: Roll with the flow. You will find meditation can be a process of uncovering what's beneath the surface. For negative emotions, you can try seeing yourself from an outside perspective, disconnect from it being yours, give compassion, and move on or release in any way you feel necessary (crying, laughing, smiling, yelling).

Tip 8: Impatience for Results

This one I struggled with. I wanted to learn how to have out-of-body experiences, reach trance states, and go into my subconscious too quickly. It made me frustrated, upset, and sometimes dislike the practice overall.

Solution: The benefits of meditation, alongside getting into the deeper work that comes from it, requires practice. By having the intention and goal to stay consistent and complete the meditation session, rather than the results you want, you will cultivate a strong practice that will give you what you need.

Meditation Techniques and Practices

In this section I'll be giving you some beginning practices you can follow with more tips for creating a custom practice for yourself, alongside different types of meditations you can utilize for your own purposes.

For many meditations, it's important to purely "feel" within our body (interoception) or visualize the intention without using words. Oftentimes when we think in our heads, we also think words alongside what we visualize. The goal to get deeper into the subconscious is to find the space in between words. This is known as the Gap, a space of pure consciousness in present awareness where the mind is still. It is a place devoid of thoughts, allowing inner wisdom to arise from silence.

An example of this is "This Statement." There are three parts: "(This)(Gap)(Statement)."

This example shows the "gap" or blank space that is in between our thoughts.

The goal is to be able to easily access the Gap between words, and with practice, it becomes easier. As we become more attuned with meditation, you'll be able to relax deeper, focus purely on your intention, and get more out of it.

When I first began to meditate, most of the time I was lying down, listening to Enya (a favorite artist of mine), and doing my best to focus on my breath. It was only after two months of consistent practice every day that I began to wander into the realms of experiencing the gap, entering into dream states consciously, and getting into the deeper benefits of meditation.

To begin, we will start with the most basic meditation you can do. You can create this practice in any way you like, but here is what I recommend:

- Pick a time either right after you wake up or before going to sleep to do your meditation. Your mind is most suggestible then, and it is easier to enter into a relaxed state, one that is in between the waking and dreaming consciousness.

    (I find it being a bonus when going to sleep, as I will fall asleep, which is fine for me.)

- You can sit or lie down. Use any props you may require or want. What is important is that you have a straight spine. If you're sitting, try not to hunch over.
- Start with a minimum of ten minutes. If you find this difficult, you can always do five-minute meditations. I find it takes me

fifteen to twenty minutes to settle in and allow the breath to calm and get you into your parasympathetic nervous system (rest and digest, calm state of being). Regardless of where you start, work your way up to ten minutes, fifteen, twenty, etc. The end goal should be being comfortable with thirty-minute-plus sessions. The deep work can take multiple hours.

- Set your intention. This can be an infinite number of things. While I have a practice I regularly do, I also have specific meditations depending on the situation or what I'm trying to accomplish. An intention of completing your practice and allowing whatever happens to happen is a great one to utilize.

- Do your best to have zero expectations on what will happen. While "mystical" things can occur, it's about being consistent in the practice to get better over time. It took me a few months to really nail it down and get consistent results. For some people, it's easier. For others, not so much. Commit to the practice and the results will follow.

- Seven seconds in, pause. Seven seconds out, pause. Repeat. This is the ideal breath to utilize. Different meditations may call for something different. Don't focus too much on counting it out; rather, take full deep breaths.

- How you choose to do your breath is up to you. Nose breathing is ideal and has amazing benefits. Different meditations and goals may want you to do specific types of breathing. Inhaling through your nose and breathing out through your mouth is another option, or only mouth breathing. Really, whatever works for you in the beginning is best. If you have a specific meditation that calls for specific breathing patterns, utilize that.

With that out of the way, let's hop into different techniques that you can utilize.

Mindfulness Meditation: Presence in Breath and Sensation

- Find a comfortable seated position, eyes gently closed.
- Take a moment to notice the natural rhythm of your breath.
- Turn your attention to the sensations in your body, observing without judgment.
- Acknowledge any thoughts or feelings that arise, then refocus on your breath.

Transcendental Meditation: Mantra of Stillness

- Sit comfortably and close your eyes.
- Begin to silently repeat a chosen mantra in your mind.
- Let the mantra gently guide you beyond thought, into stillness.
- If thoughts intrude, return softly to the mantra.
- Finish by sitting quietly for a couple of minutes before opening your eyes.

A mantra is a phrase you repeat to yourself during meditation. There are many you can choose from different cultures or practices, such as "Om Shanti" meaning "Peace." A good mantra to use is one that you have a personal connection with, that brings gratitude, ease, confidence to yourself.

Loving-Kindness Meditation: Circles of Compassion

- Begin in a relaxed pose, breathing into your heart space.
- Visualize someone you love and mentally send them well-wishes.
- Gradually extend these feelings to yourself, strangers, and even those you may have difficulty with.

- End by envisioning these waves of love and kindness expanding outward infinitely.

Basic Meditation:

- Lie or sit down with your eyes open.
- Take a deep slow inhale until you're at max capacity. Exhale slowly.
- Repeat three times.
- Close your eyes on the third exhale.
- Start deep breathing. Seven seconds in, pause. Seven seconds out, pause.
- Focus on your breath, alongside the sensation of your stomach and chest falling and rising.
- If your mind wanders, refocus on your breath.

The goal of this meditation is to work on getting into a relaxed state, alongside focusing on something that can distract your monkey brain from activating too much. This is perfect for meditation beginners.

You can also utilize visualizations, such as imagining with each breath in, a bright white light that fills you with calm, love, joy, gratitude and with each exhale, you release any stored negative energy, stress, etc. you may be having.

Basic Body Scan for Relaxation:

- Begin in a comfortable seated or prone position. Close your eyes and take a few deep breaths to settle in.
- Start at the top of your head. Notice any sensations, tension, or relaxation. Visualize each part of your body becoming lighter with each breath.
- Slowly move your attention down through your body—your neck, shoulders, arms, chest, abdomen, hips, legs, all the way to your toes.

- Spend a few moments on each area, breathing into any tension you notice, and exhaling it away.
- Finish by visualizing a wave of relaxation sweeping from head to toe.

This meditation is great for relaxation but gets you into practicing your interoception, which is having an awareness of your internal body (heartbeat, chest or diaphragm moving, pains or aches within you, etc.)

Energizing Morning Body Scan:

- Sit or stand with your spine straight, eyes open or closed.
- Begin with three deep, invigorating breaths, feeling your chest and belly expand and contract.
- Direct your attention to your feet. Wiggle your toes, feeling the energy moving in your feet.
- Gradually scan up the body, imagining a bright, energizing light filling each part as you focus on it—calves, knees, thighs, and so on.
- When you reach your head, imagine the light radiating outward, leaving you feeling refreshed and ready to start your day.

Cleansing Waterfall Visualization Meditation:

- Begin seated or lying comfortably with eyes closed.
- Imagine a clear, gentle waterfall in a serene environment.
- With each inhale, feel the water's mist, and with each exhale, visualize the waterfall washing over you.
- Envision the water cleansing away all negativity and stress.
- If overwhelmed, see the water carrying it away, leaving you refreshed.
- Conclude with a deep breath, feeling purified and light.

Heart-Brain Coherence Meditation:

I discussed this meditation in a Chapter 9 but want to emphasize how impactful it can be. Your heart and brain are uniquely connected, and by utilizing this meditation you can create coherence in your brain, which creates coherence in your life. This meditation is perfect for dealing with elevated emotions, finding gratitude, uncovering the best choice for a specific action and of course...is great for your heart and brain connection. You can find many guided versions of this meditation on YouTube and get a more detailed rundown of its benefits from the Heart Math Institute, Gregg Braden, and other resources online.

I use this method for starting my meditation. Once I feel a deep, elevated emotion of joy or gratitude throughout my body, I begin to do manifestation work.

- Sit or lie comfortably with your eyes closed.
- Inhale for five to seven seconds, pause. Exhale for five to seven seconds, pause. Repeat.
- Focus on visualizing a strand that connects your heart to your brain and creating that connection between the two.
  - (If you find this difficult, try placing a hand over your heart, or you may notice many cultures will use prayer hands, thumbs touching their heart to make that connection.)
- After establishing a connection, focus and visualize on a person, place or situation that brings you great joy, gratitude, or another elevated positive emotion.
- Feel that emotion throughout your body and let it wash over you until you're existing within this emotion.
- Sit with this for as long as you may need.

You can set your intention for the session and also seek answers through this state of awareness.

Each of these meditations are great for starting out and can help you with the foundations of a meditation practice. Another resource you can utilize is the app Headspace, it offers tons of meditations, for all sorts of different areas in your life, alongside a beginner course that will teach you the fundamentals of meditation.

You can also find many guided versions of these meditations on YouTube. The ultimate goal is to make it a daily practice and tool you can utilize.

I encourage you to try out one of these meditations as your activity for this section.

Benefits of Breathwork

Breathwork is a powerful tool that can be used for many purposes. Without realizing it, we practice breathwork every day. Depending on how we breathe, it creates a physiological response within our body. We can use our breath as a tool to create change within our physiology, often referred to as a bottom-up method (utilizing physiology to change our mental state).

Depending on where we breathe within our body, it has an effect on us. Shallow breathing is often associated with chest breathing. When we breathe through our chest it typically causes less oxygen exchange alongside feelings of stress and tension.

When we use your diaphragm to breathe, also known as belly breathing, it is associated with deeper fuller breaths, more efficient oxygen exchange, and promotes relaxation and calmness within the body.

We also breathe through our backs and alongside our rib cage. A deep full breath could be starting with the belly, expanding the chest, expanding the rib cage and out the back, then releasing. Breathwork is a great way to increase your own interoception.

Some of the benefits of breathwork are:

Stress Reduction

- A meta-analysis has demonstrated that breathwork interventions are associated with lower levels of self-reported stress compared to non-breathwork controls, with a small-to-medium effect size. This suggests that breathwork can effectively reduce stress. (Fincham et al., 2023)

Improvement of Mental Health

- Breathwork practices are reported to have therapeutic potential to improve mental health, with significant effect sizes found for reducing anxiety and depressive symptoms in randomized-controlled trials. These findings suggest that breathwork can be a valuable non-pharmacological intervention for mental health issues.

Enhanced Autonomic Nervous System Function

- Slow-paced breathing practices, often included in breathwork, have been associated with increased heart-rate variability (HRV), which is indicative of a more resilient stress-response system. High HRV is considered beneficial as it reflects robust responses to environmental demands and is associated with improved health, as well as better emotional and cognitive functioning.

Improved Physiological Communication

⊚ Modifying breathing patterns is known to rapidly influence brain regions that regulate behavior, thought, and emotion. Slow breathing, in particular, can lead to synchrony of brain waves, which may enable more effective communication across different brain regions. Such entrainment of brain activity could have significant implications for cognitive and emotional processes.

Easier to Get into Deep Meditative States

⊚ Through breathwork we can access deep states of relaxation that could take much longer to reach through a meditation practice. This is one of my favorite aspects of breathwork, as anyone can do it and get amazing results quickly without having much practice.

There are many more benefits you can dive deeper into. I highly recommend *Becoming the Iceman* by Wim Hof. It gives you amazing insight into his form of breathwork alongside how great cold exposure is.

Alongside these benefits, breathwork is associated with deep emotional release. These may come out as laughs, cries, yelling or anger, physical movement, somatic experiences (feeling heat, cold, tingling, or other physical sensations), having an epiphany in a specific situation, releasing emotions from a traumatic experience or event in your life, and other forms of release.

It is always important to practice breathwork in a safe and supportive environment that is non-judgmental. If you work with a facilitator, they should be able to hold space and help guide and support you through these emotional releases that may occur. These physical releases are often a crucial step in healing and can lead to significant personal growth and emotional well-being.

Breathwork Tips

- **Create a Safe Space:** Ensure you're in a comfortable and private environment where you won't be disturbed. This safety can facilitate a deeper experience. Make sure there are no objects you may accidentally fall into. Certain forms of breathwork may cause you to feel dizzy or light-headed.
- **Find a Comfortable Position:** Whether you choose to sit or lie down, make sure your body is supported so that you can fully relax without holding any tension.
- **Set an Intention:** Before beginning, decide what you want to achieve with your breathwork session, whether it's relaxation, energy, or emotional release.
- **Begin with Normal Breathing:** Start by observing your natural breath to become present and centered before you engage in any specific breathing patterns.
- **Use a Guided Audio:** Especially for beginners, having a guided breathwork audio can help keep you on track and enhance the experience.
- **Don't Force the Breath:** Allow your breath to flow naturally and comfortably. Avoid straining or forcing it, which can cause tension rather than release.
- **Stay Hydrated:** Drink water before and after your breathwork session to help facilitate the detoxification process that deep breathing can initiate.
- **Notice Physical Sensations:** Pay attention to the sensations in your body. Breathwork can cause tingling or light-headedness. If it becomes too intense, return to your normal breathing pattern.

- **Be Patient with Yourself:** If your mind wanders or you find the process challenging, gently bring your focus back to your breath without judgment.
- **Integrate Rest:** After a breathwork session, give yourself time to rest and integrate the experience. This might include journaling or simply lying quietly.
- **Listen to Your Body:** If you experience any discomfort, modify the practice to suit your needs or stop the exercise altogether.
- **Regular Practice:** Consistency is key in breathwork. Regular practice can enhance the benefits and your proficiency with the techniques.
- **Seek Professional Guidance:** For those new to breathwork or working through significant emotional blocks, professional guidance from a certified breathwork therapist can provide support and safety.

Breathwork Techniques

Breathwork is an ancient practice, backed by modern science. It holds the key to unlocking physical, emotional and spiritual benefits alongside fostering a deep connection with ourselves.

In the following section we will be exploring a variety of breathwork techniques, each with their own unique purpose from calming the mind to shifting into the parasympathetic nervous system and fostering emotional release.

I invite you to approach these exercises with an open heart and mind, to discover the power of your breath. Remember, while breathwork can be practiced by many, it is not suitable for everyone. Please refer to the safety disclaimer in the beginning of the book before beginning, to ensure a safe and beneficial practice.

Diaphragmatic Breathing: To activate the diaphragm for deep, relaxing breaths that engage the full capacity of the lungs.

- Find a comfortable seated or prone position.
- Place one hand on your chest and the other on your belly.
- Breathe in slowly through your nose, feeling your belly rise more than your chest.
- Exhale through pursed lips, feeling the belly fall.
- Continue for three to five minutes, focusing on the belly's rise and fall.

Box Breathing: To activate the diaphragm for deep, relaxing breaths that engage the full capacity of the lungs.

- Sit upright in a comfortable chair with your feet flat on the floor.
- Close your eyes and take a few normal breaths to prepare.
- Inhale to the count of four, filling your lungs completely.
- Hold your breath for another count of four.
- Exhale slowly to the count of four, emptying your lungs entirely.
- Hold your lungs empty for a count of four.
- Repeat the cycle for three to five minutes.

4-7-8 Breathing: To reduce anxiety, help with sleep, and manage cravings.

- Sit or lie in a comfortable position with a straight back.
- Place the tip of your tongue behind your upper front teeth.
- Exhale completely through your mouth, making a whoosh sound.
- Close your mouth and inhale quietly through your nose to a count of four.
- Hold your breath for a count of seven.

- Exhale completely through your mouth, making a whoosh sound to a count of eight.
- Repeat the cycle four times.

Lion's Breath: To relieve stress, tension in the face and improve vocal articulation.

- Come to a comfortable seated position with your spine straight.
- Press your palms against your knees with fingers spread wide.
- Inhale deeply through your nose.
- Open your mouth wide, stick out your tongue towards your chin, and exhale forcefully with a "ha" sound.
- Repeat for several breaths, then sit quietly for a few moments.

Tummo Breathing: To generate inner warmth and increase vitality by directing breath and energy through the body's central channels.

- Begin by sitting in a comfortable meditation posture with your back straight.
- Close your eyes and bring your attention to your breath.
- Start by inhaling deeply through your belly, then chest. Letting go almost immediately once you have a full breath, but do not force the air out.
- Do this for as many breaths as you want, I recommend aiming to do 3-12 per round.
- On your final breath, inhale deeply through the nose, filling the belly, then the chest.
- Swallow the air and push it out through your belly, expanding your abdomen.
- Hold the breath for twenty to thirty seconds, or until you can no longer hold it.

- Exhale slowly and fully through the mouth, make sure your lips are pursed, as if you were blowing through a straw. If there was a feather in front of you, you wouldn't be able to blow it away for how slow and gentle your breath is.
- After exhaling, hold the breath out and contract your abdominal muscles to push any remaining air out, but without straining.
- Repeat this cycle for several rounds, starting with what feels comfortable for you.

Managing Stress Levels

Stress is an inherent part of life. It can be beneficial for many of our goals, but when stress becomes chronic, it starts to have a negative impact on our lives. It can drain our energy levels, contribute to disharmony, and throw us off balance. Understanding the physiological basis of stress and learning how to manage it is a vital part to maintaining health and alignment. We will begin by learning the differences between our parasympathetic and sympathetic nervous systems.

The Parasympathetic and Sympathetic Nervous System:

The sympathetic nervous system is often referred to as a "fight or flight" response. It prepares the body to deal with perceived threats by releasing hormones such as adrenaline and cortisol. This increases your heart rate and diverts energy to essential functions in the body.

In acute situations, this is crucial for us to escape danger, dodge out of the way of an obstacle while driving, and become hyper aware of our surroundings and other situations. Many humans today experience chronic activation of stress, which leads to health issues and fatigue.

The parasympathetic nervous system, on the other hand, is the "rest and digest" response. It helps the body conserve energy, promotes relaxation, digestion, and healing. Activating this system reduces the stress hormones and creates a calming effect on the body.

As we mentioned in the mindset chapter 8, we can take a stress-is-enhancing mindset, this allows us to access the positive outcomes in which an acute response can be beneficial for us, pooling resources to achieve a given outcome.

Types of Stressors

Stress is caused by a multitude of different stressors. A stressor is a stimulus that challenges the body's homeostasis. Stressors can be psychological, physical, or emotional. The outcome of the stress depends on the way each person perceives the situation and then reacts. Stressors can be defined in multiple ways. I'll be writing on internal and external stressors.

Internal stressors are self-induced, often including a person's attitudes, beliefs, perceptions, and expectations. This can be internal worries, perceived lack of control influenced by fears, past memories, anticipation of what may unfold, and other situations.

External stressors, on the other hand, come from outside events, experiences, and situations. These can include financial worries, major life changes, physical environment, physical pain or injury, household commitments, and other factors.

Physiological Effects of Stress

Acute Stress (short-term):

- Increased heart rate
- Increased blood pressure
- Increased respiration rate

- Increased alertness
- Rising blood glucose levels
- Slower digestion
- Reduced kidney function

Chronic Stress (long-term):

- Altered emotions
- Reproductive problems
- Increased risk for osteoporosis
- Increased insulin resistance
- Chronic inflammation
- Gastrointestinal issues
- Weight gain
- Memory impairment
- Cardiovascular dysfunction
- Chronic pain
- Headaches

As you can see, the acute response is our body pooling resources to potentially deal with a threat, while chronic stress will exacerbate a wide variety of issues with no end in sight.

In modern times, these threats are typically, making it to work on time, meeting a deadline, giving a presentation, social interactions and a wide range of activities which then trigger our response. On top of this, unlike escaping from a wild animal, these stressors are long-standing or recurring on a daily basis. As we try to do more with less time, we find ourselves experiencing chronic stress.

Building Resilience in the Face of Stress

At its core, resilience is what allows us to deal with stressors that we may face throughout our lives and come out of it not only unscathed but enhanced. This is a process of being able to adapt in the face of adversity, trauma, threats, or other sources of stress. We build this by adopting a stress-is-enhancing mindset, growth-based mindset or positive personality. Ultimately seeing stressors as an opportunity for growth.

The way we build resilience is through a variety of different components:

- **Emotional awareness:** Recognizing one's own thoughts, feelings, behaviors and how they interconnect is crucial for navigating the highs and lows of stress with ease.
- **Perseverance:** Sticking to the goal and changing the plan when necessary is a hallmark of resilience. The more we practice consistency and seek proactive solutions to the problems, the more resilience we can cultivate.
- **Optimism:** Being able to see the positives in every situation and keeping your focus on the highest possibility can greatly influence outcomes. Optimism isn't about ignoring the difficulties and challenges, rather maintaining a sense of hope and overcoming them.
- **Flexibility:** Resilient individuals are able to adapt to new circumstances with ease. They are open to alternative pathways to achieving their goals and shift when needed.
- **Support Networks:** I cannot stress this enough! Strong relationships and networks with individuals who are on the same path as you can provide emotional or practical help as absolutely invaluable.

Strategies to Enhance Resilience

There are a variety of strategies we can utilize to enhance our resilience in the face of stress.

- **Self-Care:** This includes regular physical exercise, adequate sleep, and proper nutrition

- **Mindfulness Practice:** Being in the present moment allows you to focus on the stressor at hand and meet it with compassion and understanding.
- **Skill Development:** The more skills we have, the more confidence we have. Whatever you feel you may be lacking or need extra information on, start to create a plan to develop that skill.
- **Purpose and Goals:** Setting and working towards goals that bring out your internal fire and are aligned with your big-ticket items will allow you to see the big picture and push through many challenges that arise.
- **Utilizing Mindset Frameworks:** Utilizing many of the frameworks we've talked about, such as the growth-based and stress-is-enhancing mindset, will allow you to take a different approach and see a new perspective on the situation.

The Silver Lining of Stress: Flow and Performance

When we hear about stress in our daily lives, it's often pictured as a negative aspect. As we now know, it has many positive benefits. When we can channel our stress correctly, it can be a powerful friend in achieving peak performance and activating the flow state.

The stress-performance connection as seen through the Yerkes-Dodson Law posits that performance increases with physiological arousal (stress), but only up until a certain point. When stress levels become too high, performance decreases, yet when they are too low, performance also decreases. The key to finding a balance between the effort you put in on your performance to the level of stress you perceive which creates the optimal level for performance. This allows you to access the flow state.

Stress is also a catalyst for the flow state. This is a concept introduced by psychologist Mihaly Csikszentmihalyi. The flow state describes a state of complete immersion in an activity where time seems to stand still, and a person is fully absorbed in the present moment. This can be marked by the amount of skill you have for a given challenge. If the challenge is too high, without having proper skill, you may experience fear and anxiety. If you have a high amount of skill, but little challenge in the activity, you may experience boredom. In order to reach the flow state, we need enough skill to be able to meet a challenge that is just hard enough for us to be able to succeed.

An example of this is a runner who has been training all year to complete a marathon. They are well-prepared for the race, yet the challenge is completing the entire marathon, which requires endurance, strategy, resilience. Yet it is within the runner's capabilities to meet this challenge head-on due to their experiences and training. When the runner starts this marathon, they begin to experience the state of flow, listening to their body's feedback, being in the present moment, aware of their environment but detached from outside distractions.

Stress Assessment

There is a free online source I prefer to use, referred to as the Holmes and Rahe stress scale.

It can be taken for free at: www.stress.org/holmes-rahe-stress-inventory/

- What are your stress levels rated at?
- Identify your primary stress triggers. Are they work related? Personal? Environmental?
- Reflect on how you respond to stress. Do you experience any physiological symptoms?

Relaxation Techniques for Stress

We have plenty of techniques we can pull on for dealing with stress, many of which we have described in the mindset chapter and throughout the meditation and breathwork sections. We will be touching back on some of these techniques and introduce some new ones.

Deep Breathing

- Find a comfortable and quiet place to sit or lie down.
- Place one hand on your chest and the other on your belly.
- Take a slow, deep breath through your nose, allowing your belly to push your hand out. Your chest should not move.
- Breathe out through pursed lips as if you were whistling. Feel the hand on your belly go in, using it to push all the air out.
- Do this breathing three to ten times. Take your time with each breath.

Mindfulness Meditation

- Sit comfortably with your back straight and eyes closed.
- Focus on your natural breathing or on a word or "mantra" that you repeat silently.
- Allow thoughts to come and go without judgment and return to your focus on breath or mantra.
- Practice this meditation for five to ten minutes initially, gradually increasing the time.

Progressive Muscle Relaxation

- Begin by finding a comfortable position, either sitting or lying down.
- Close your eyes and take a few deep breaths to relax.

- Starting with your feet, tense the muscles as tightly as you can. Hold for a count of five, and then relax.
- Gradually work your way up through your body—legs, abdomen, back, arms, neck, and face—tensing and relaxing each muscle group.
- Spend about five to ten minutes on this exercise.

Guided Imagery

- Find a quiet, comfortable place to relax.
- Close your eyes and take a few deep breaths.
- Imagine a peaceful scene, place, or experience—this could be a beach, a mountain, a forest, or any place you find calming.
- Involve all your senses. For example, if you're at the beach, hear the waves, feel the sand, and smell the ocean.
- Stay in your scene for five to ten minutes, breathing slowly and deeply.

This can also include mindful movement such as tai chi, yoga, qigong, walking and cycling, earthing, etc.

Understanding and managing your stress levels is an important part to having long-lasting energy and overall health. Through this understanding and these practices, you can effectively balance your sympathetic and parasympathetic nervous system responses, leading to a healthier internal environment.

Think back to a time where you successfully managed your stress? What did you do? Oftentimes what works best.... Is your unique solution!

Energy Hygiene Practices

Our own energy fields are bombarded every day from environmental factors to the emotional state of others we encounter. Just as personal hygiene practices are important for health, energy hygiene is crucial for supporting our emotional and energetic well-being. Implementing simple but effective practices can help release anything that isn't serving us, improve our energy, and maintain balance.

Energy hygiene itself is referring to practices we can use to cleanse and maintain the integrity of our own personal energy fields. These practices help us clear away the "energetic debris" that can accumulate through everyday interactions and stressors.

This is great if you're dealing with many challenges throughout the day or work in an environment like massage therapists, who constantly receive energy from others and drain their own energy through bodywork on their clients. Sometimes we need to take a break, collect ourselves, and utilize practices that allow us to stay grounded. If we are not balanced ourselves, it is difficult to support others without becoming burnt out or experiencing negative effects of constantly holding space.

Daily Energy Hygiene Practices

Morning Grounding Meditation:

- Start your day with a five-minute grounding meditation. Visualize roots extending from the soles of your feet, going deep into the earth, anchoring you firmly to the ground. Breathe deeply, and with each exhalation, release any tension or negativity.

Protective Shielding:

- Envision a bubble of protective light around you after your grounding meditation. Choose a color that resonates with safety and protection for you. Intend for this shield to deflect negativity and maintain your energy purity throughout the day.

Mindful Breathing Breaks:

- Intersperse your day with mindful breathing breaks. Take a few minutes to focus solely on your breath, allowing your energy to settle and center. This practice helps in releasing accumulated stress and refocusing your energy.

Intentional Movement:

- Engage in intentional movements to keep the energy flowing through your body. This could be a brief walk, stretching, yoga, or tai chi. The goal is to prevent stagnation and promote the flow of energy.

Evening Cleansing Ritual:

- Conclude your day with an evening cleansing ritual. This can involve a warm bath infused with salts known for their energetic cleansing properties, like Himalayan or Epsom salts. Alternatively, imagine a shower washing away any dense or unwanted energies from the day.

Gratitude Reflection:

- End your day on a positive note with a gratitude reflection. Write down or mentally acknowledge at least three things you are grateful for. Gratitude elevates your energy frequency and promotes positive flow.

You can take these practices and customize them to however you may need or use any of the other techniques in the book to do so. Below, I will give you guidelines to help craft your own energy hygiene routine.

ACTIVITY: Crafting Your Routine

Identify Your Needs:

- Reflect on what parts of your day feel most energetically taxing. Is it the morning rush, midday interactions, or the evening wind-down?

Select Practices that Resonate:

- Choose from the above practices or others you may know, selecting those that you feel drawn to and that address the needs you've identified.

Establish a Schedule:

- Determine the most feasible times to integrate these practices into your daily routine. Consistency is key.

Commit to Practice:

- Commit to your chosen practices to establish a habit. Observe and note any changes in your energy levels and overall well-being.

Remember, energy hygiene practices are not one-size-fits-all. They should be personalized to fit into your lifestyle and meet your unique energetic needs. By maintaining regular energy hygiene, you can ensure that your energy remains clear, vibrant, and aligned with your highest good.

Grounding Techniques

Grounding, or earthing, is one of my favorite techniques and the most accessible to everyone. It is a practice in which you reconnect to the earth with your bare skin, typically by having your feet on the earth. This is based on earthing science, which suggests that the electrical energy from the earth can have a positive effect on your body by transferring electrons into the body.

Humans are innately a part of the world around us. We are not separate from nature, but rather deeply ingrained and built from it. There are many functions encoded in our own biology that are based around the electromagnetics of the planet, the seasons, the sunlight we get, and other universal systems.

When rubberized shoes became more available and popular, we started to stop connecting to earth in this way, which has presented problems with the provided benefits it had. Think about the last time you were barefoot on the earth. For many, it could be weeks, if not months or years since doing so.

I'll be going over the efficacy of grounding and its benefits alongside giving you some easy practices to integrate into your routines.

Efficacy of Grounding

- Improvement in Sleep, pain, and stress: A study summarized in the *Journal of Environmental and Public Health* indicates that grounding may improve sleep, normalize the day-night cortisol rhythm, reduce pain, and decrease stress by facilitating the body's electrical connectivity with the Earth's electron-rich surface (Oschman et al., 2015).
- Reduction in Blood Viscosity: A publication in the *Journal of Inflammation Research* points to grounding reducing blood viscosity, a major factor in cardiovascular disease. This effect

is significant because high blood viscosity can contribute to the risk of heart attack and stroke. (Chevalier et al., 2013).

- Anti-Inflammatory Effects: Grounding has also been called, "The universal anti-inflammatory remedy" due to its potential in reducing inflammation, an underlying factor in many chronic diseases. (Sinatra et al., 2022).

Incorporating Grounding into Your Routine

Grounding is incredibly simple to practice, and here are techniques to add into your routine:

- Direct Contact: Walk barefoot on natural surfaces like grass, soil, or sand. Aim for at least thirty minutes of exposure. This is a perfect activity to combine with meditation, reading, walking a pet, or heading into nature.
- Grounding Equipment: There are many types of grounding mats, sheets, and bands you can purchase online that plug into the grounding slot in electrical outlets. It's important to use a multimeter to check whether the outlets grounding port is doing what it should. Earthing.com has some top-notch gear, or you can find competitors on Amazon for a better price.

You could even make your own by getting some low-gauge copper, connecting it to yourself or an object you connect with and shoving the other end into the ground. They also make handy grounding tethers for this you can find on Amazon.

On YouTube, you can find a documentary called "The Earthing Movie: The Remarkable Science of Grounding (full documentary)." It has an incredible deep dive into earthing, the science behind it, and is a good one-stop shop to start your research.

As with anything, I suggest a consistent practice in order to get consistent results. Get outside and start to ground yourself as you walk on your journey to self-alignment.

Protecting Your Energy

Every day, we encounter situations that can throw us off balance, whether that's environmental, social, or internal. Learning to protect our energy is essential to preserving emotional well-being, mental clarity, and overall health. Energy work isn't just for the Reiki masters or yogi gurus; it's a practical tool that anyone can utilize.

The goal with protecting your energy is learning how to set proper boundaries and practices with yourself and the people around you.

As you may know, you will end up like the five people you spend the most time with, their habits, behaviors and energy being so strong it quite literally shapes you like them. You may also encounter negative individuals throughout your day or help others who are experiencing lower vibrational emotions (sadness, depression, anger, jealousy, etc.).

Strategies for Energy Protection

- **Awareness:** Recognize situations and individuals that drain your energy. Having that awareness is a step towards protecting yourself.
- **Boundaries:** Learn to say no. It's okay to limit the time spent with individuals that drain your energy or to decline commitments that don't align with your well-being.
- **Selective Sharing:** Be mindful of the information you share with others. Oversharing can sometimes lead to our energy being invested in or taken by others without us realizing it.
- **Positive Surroundings:** Surround yourself with positive individuals and environments, those who are aligned with

your journey in their own way and a space that supports your growth.

- **Self-Care:** Regular self-care practices can help replenish your energy, whether it's a bath, meditation, exercise, journaling, or any hobby that brings you joy.

You may want to learn how to use the subtle energy within us and all around us to also protect you. This can be done through intention and visualization.

Energy Shielding Exercise:

- Sit or stand comfortably in a quiet place where you won't be disturbed.
- Begin by taking deep, slow breaths. Inhale positivity and exhale negativity.
- Visualize a bubble or shield of light forming around you. Choose a color that represents protection and strength to you—many find white, gold, or blue effective.
- As you visualize this shield, set the intention that this is a barrier that only allows positive energy in and keeps negative energy out.
- Reinforce your shield by affirming its presence. You might say, "I am surrounded by protective light, and only positive energy can enter my space."

A mentor of mine shared with me a mantra he received from his teacher that is a powerful tool I whip out whenever I'm feeling off balance or getting too deep into a negative frame of mind. Repeat this as many times as you need: "I do not consent to any dark forces or negative energy invading my mind space or auric field."

Other Tools for Energy Protection

Crystals and Gemstones: Besides being absolutely beautiful pieces to have around you, you can utilize crystals as a form of protection and pull from their unique energetic properties.

Here are some crystals you can use:

- Black tourmaline: A powerful stone for protection. It is incredibly grounding and helps clear and repel negative energy.
- Clear Quartz: A well-balanced crystal for both repelling negative energy and attracting positive energy.
- Citrine: Also known as a powerful stone for manifesting, it can absorb negative energy and transmute it into positive.
- Selenite: Used to recharge your own energy and balance out the energy of any crystals.

There are many different stones you can use for a variety of reasons. What's most important is how to use them. Before you can utilize any crystal, you want to clear its energy, which can be done by placing it on a slab of selenite, charging it in the sun or moonlight, smudging it with palo santo or sage, burying it in the earth for a day, or a variety of other ways.

Once the crystal has been rebalanced, you can hold it in your hands, create an intention you want this stone to help you with and then visualize your intention as energy that is coming through your body, into your hands and into the stone. It's important to program your crystals and cleanse them regularly.

If you're interested in learning more about crystals, I highly recommend the book "The Book of Stones – Who They Are & What They Teach" by Robert simmons & Naisha Ahsian.

Energy Cleaners & Balancers

Orgonite: Orgone, discovered by Wilhelm Reich, is a method of using inorganic and organic matter stacked in a particular way that absorbs negative electromagnetic frequencies and transmutes them into less harmful frequencies. You can create your own or purchase them. What's important is making sure you buy from a trusted source.

Many orgone you find online are more so resin projects with crystals in them that claim to be orgonite pieces. You can set up orgone pieces next to high EMF electronics, under your bed, around your workspace, or anywhere that you spend quite a bit of time in. I prefer to have an orgone necklace alongside setting them up around the house in key locations.

One of my good friends Nick (@ascenion_orgone on Instagram) makes beautiful pieces but also provides valuable information on learning the difference between basic resin pieces and proper orgone generators.

Smudging: Palo Santo has been used for over a thousand years by Indigenous tribes of South America, referred to as "holy wood" in Spanish. It is traditionally used during sacred rituals and healing ceremonies to cleanse the air of negative energy and aid in the resolution of conflictual situations.

Sage used for smudging traces itself back two thousand years. It is an Indigenous American practice, widely used by Native Americans. This involves burning it to bless, protect and cleanse negative energy.

Burn either in whatever space you want to cleanse, whether it's yourself, an object, environment etc. Have your intention set to ridding anything that is low vibrational and keep your space protected.

Cultivating a Nurturing Environment

The spaces we inhabit play a crucial role in shaping our energy, mood, and overall health. No doubt you've been in environments you found beneficial for your growth, making you feel relaxed, or others that are more disruptive or even off putting to your well-being. By cultivating an environment that nurtures and balances our energy, we can enhance our sense of peace, creativity and ultimately have a space for maximum growth.

Our environments are not only physical spaces but hold energy that can affect us for better or worse. Disorganized, or dreary spaces will lead us to feel unease and stagnation, while clean and harmonious spaces can uplift and inspire us.

You can take a look at someone's room, inside their car, their kitchen, and if there is a good amount of disorganization, it can be a signifier that they themselves are disorganized internally. This is a great example of what we have within us will project outwardly, and in this case into our physical environment.

By cleaning up, decluttering, and ultimately creating a space that you find beneficial for your own activities or growth, you will also foster a clearer headspace with less distractions. Different rooms can have different elements that can help support the function of that room.

If you have a television or computer in your bedroom, you're now creating a space that cultivates energy and thoughts surrounding that rather than sleep. While if your bedroom is set up purely for sleeping and relaxing activities, your body and mind will associate the room with calming energy to help you get to bed and release the stressors of the day.

Tips for Creating an Energy-Balanced Environment

- Declutter: Start by decluttering your space. Removing clutter will help create a distraction-free environment that makes it easier to think and simply exist

- Natural Elements: Incorporate water elements or plants to your environment. There are many plants that are suited for indoors and help create an oxygen-rich environment such as:
    - Snake plant
    - Spider plant
    - Aloe vera (good for bathrooms as it absorbs odors)
    - Money tree (known for its good luck)
    - Bamboo palm
    - Dragon tree
    - Pithos

- Color Therapy: Different colors support different moods. Blue and green for calming, yellow for creativity or cheerfulness.

- Aromatherapy: Different aromas help create different internal changes, and if you use a specific one, say, for sleep, when your body smells it, it will react by becoming calmer and getting ready for bed. You can buy all sorts of diffusers online and get yourself an organic essential oil pack and experiment with what works for you.

- Personal Touches: Make it *your* room! Add in photos, artwork, I that fits *you* and the function of the room.
    - My office has a makeshift vision board with photos that I'm manifesting in my life to remind me of where I'm heading and support the work I do.

- Soundscapes: Set up music that helps support you and the function of the room, or if you work better without it...don't!

Let's assess your environment through a quick exercise.

- Assess Your Space: Take a walk through your personal or home environment. How does each area make you feel? Take note of spaces that make you feel good and those that don't.
- Identify Improvements: List changes that could enhance each space's energy. This could be as simple as rearranging furniture for better flow, adding plants, or changing the lighting.
- Plan Modifications: Prioritize the changes based on impact and feasibility. Create a step-by-step plan for implementing these modifications.
- Take Action: Start with the simplest changes and work your way through your list. Remember, even small changes can make a significant difference.
- Reflect and Adjust: After making changes, spend time in your newly arranged space. Reflect on how the modifications have altered the energy. Feel free to adjust as needed until you find the right balance.

By being mindful of the energy in our environments and taking steps to cultivate spaces that support and nurture us, we can enhance our overall well-being and create sanctuaries that serve as foundations for our best self.

Conclusion

As we close out this chapter on energy work, it's important to reflect on everything we've been through so far. We've explored a variety of topics, from practical tools such as meditation and breathwork to learning how to create a nurturing environment. The journey isn't just learning these techniques but applying them in our lives to deepen our internal connection to our highest self and the world around us.

At the heart of energy work lies the power of intention. Whether you're grounding yourself, cleansing a crystal, or rebalancing your environment, it's intention that fuses these activities with meaning. Setting clear, positive intentions allows you to align most closely with your desired outcomes.

Remember, energy work is highly personal. What works for you may not work for another. Trusting your intuition and embracing the practices that feel right for you is key to this work. It is about taking these tools to balance and harmonize yourself in a way that honors your own unique being.

Moving forward, you will carry with you the knowledge of the underlying energy that is within everything and the tools that benefit you the most. When we take accountability for ourselves in every aspect to cultivate our own self-growth, this becomes a powerful tool that will enhance our lives.

Take care of your body. It's the only place you have to live.

- JIM ROHN

11

Insight into the Three Pillars – Movement Nutrition and Sleep

In this chapter, we will be diving into foundational elements that have a huge impact on our mental state, physiology, and allow us to stay focused and aligned: nutrition, movement, and sleep. This will involve bringing awareness to these three pillars, useful tips, techniques that help support you.

Movement, nutrition, and sleep play a critical role in maintaining our physical health, managing stress, and boosting our mood. Regular physical exercise isn't only for our body's well-being but our mind. Imagine your car without proper maintenance. Eventually, it starts to break down, parts need to be replaced, it functions worse and worse. Without proper maintenance of our body, the exact same thing happens. Even more so important is the residual effects it has on increasing our cognition, preventing disease and injury, alongside being able to do activities with ease.

Nutrition is our fuel, the very source that powers all bodily functions. It's not about eating for pleasure through ultra-processed, highly palatable foods. Rather, it's about nourishing ourselves with the right foods that provide essential nutrients to thrive. The choices we make in our diet have massive implications to our overall mood, health, and energy levels. While this is not a book about nutrition, we will go over information to make more informed choices about the food we eat.

Finally, we have sleep hygiene, an often-overlooked component in our always-on-the-go culture asking of us to work longer hours and our technological advancements that lead us to spend all our time addicted to cheap dopamine releases. Quality sleep is crucial for our body's repair processes, cognitive functioning, emotional regulation, and so much more. We will cover the importance of good sleep practices, creating a great environment for restful sleep, and techniques to help with sleep quality.

As with the car analogy we used above, without proper maintenance of these critical areas of our health, we will be always in a challenging battle to create our most aligned life if we ourselves are not aligned physically or mentally. While yes, you do not need any of these components to be successful, why drive a car that is breaking down, keeps you at a lower throttle and is unreliable, when you can use simple and effective habits to make the journey that much easier?

Movement: The Keystone to Vitality

I've encountered many individuals, including myself at one point, who believed they were confined to being a certain way. The notion suggests you're trapped with the life handed to you: you 'aren't fit, smart, funny, creative, or any other trait or situation you find yourself in. However, life does not pigeonhole us into a single identity we must adhere to. Instead, change is one of the universe's constant forces. Life is not about who you *are* but who you *become*—and becoming is a journey that lasts a lifetime.

Exercise epitomizes this principle, guiding the wisdom I choose to embrace. Our journey begins by recognizing that things 'aren't as we wish them to be, either physically or mentally. Then, through our vision, we catch a glimpse of who we can become. Through intentional action (exercise), we can bring to life the reality we choose.

Exercise teaches us that through intentional work and discipline, we can achieve the goals we dream o'. It's not only about gaining general wellness or a pleasing appearance; it brings about a comprehensive shift in our productivity, focus, mental health, and management of chronic diseases. It aids in proper hormone production and offers much more. Regular movement is among the best practices to forge your most aligned life.

The Significance of Regular Movement

Regular exercise is the cornerstone of maintaining our physical health, acting as a powerful deterrent against chronic diseases. Right now, it is estimated that 117 million people, an estimated one in two people, have at least one chronic health condition. This may be heart disease, obesity, hypertension, cancer, and that one in four adults has two or more chronic conditions (Ward et al., 2014).

Engaging in consistent regular exercise fortifies the heart, enhances lung capacity, and strengthens the musculoskeletal system. This helps reduce the risk of many chronic diseases such as diabetes, heart disease, osteoporosis. Exercise also plays a huge role in regulating body weight and metabolic functions, which has been greatly documented. This offers a profound and simple way to bring back balance into your life.

Not only this, but it's found that some of the other general benefits you gain from regular exercise, activity, or both is increased cognitive functioning, feelings of well-being, physical function and independent living (in older adults), and performance of work, recreational, and sport activities. It also helps decrease mortality, morbidity, anxiety and depression, risks for falls and injuries, and risk factors for coronary artery disease. 'What's great about physical activity is that it's found to have a dose-response relationship—the more we do, the greater the benefits. As we know, as above so below, if you are physically inactive you will receive many of the decreased benefits. If you're completely physically inactive, a simple walk is better than no activity at all. More activity up until a point is also better than some. In fact, if you're completely sedentary, you will benefit significantly from a modest increase in physical activity in terms of your improvement in health status. (Liguory et al., 2022)

Mental Health, Stress Reduction, and Mood Improvement

Physical activity not only enhances your physiological health but is found to have amazing benefits when it comes to depression and anxiety, stress reduction, and overall mood improvement. Last year, a large analysis of meta-studies found that exercise is more beneficial for conditions such as anxiety and depression than standard psychotherapy or medicine and that all forms of exercise produced significant mental health benefits. (Singh et al., 2023)

Research led by Dr. Ben Singh highlights that engaging in physical activity is 1.5 times more effective in reducing mild to moderate symptoms of depression, psychological stress, and anxiety compared to cognitive behavioral therapy or medication.

Physical activity will also release endorphins, which can greatly affect your overall mood and thought patterns. There have been countless times I've not wanted to go on a run, to the gym, etc., and I'll force my body to make moves in that direction. By the time I'm done with my workout or halfway through, I feel such relief that I put in the effort and also feel fantastic crushing it out. If you can show up for yourself, you've achieved the ultimate goal and will be rewarded by pushing through.

General Benefits of Exercise

Exercise offers numerous benefits, enhancing cognitive functioning across various life stages. This includes improvements in memory, processing speed, and executive functions, which are crucial for focus and cognitive performance. Regular moderate to vigorous exercise has been shown to reduce the risk of cognitive impairment, including Alzheimer's disease (Erickson et al., 2019).

Numerous studies demonstrate the significant impact of physical activity and cardiovascular exercises, such as walking, on productivity. Workers who incorporate exercise into their routine often find it easier to manage and feel less stressed throughout their day.

My favorite aspect of physical exercise is the immediate benefits it provides from the very first day. With each workout and consistent effort, you gain increasing benefits. This is one of the most effective ways to practice self-love and enjoy remarkable advantages while feeling good.

You'll also start to have more energy throughout your day and access positive thoughts and feelings more readily. Pursuing this path of self-realization and fulfillment inevitably presents challenges. However, I emphasize repeatedly that regular exercise equips you to meet these challenges more easily or manage the stress associated with them. Instead of being overwhelmed, you can perceive challenges for what they are and move beyond them.

One of the most immediate rewards of consistent exercise is the significant improvement in sleep quality. As we exert ourselves physically, we pave the way for deeper, more restorative sleep. This isn't just about sleeping longer but about enhancing the quality of sleep we get. Exercise helps regulate our body's internal clock, easing us into a natural sleep rhythm that leaves us refreshed and alert upon waking.

Energy levels too see a remarkable uptick with regular exercise. This might seem counterintuitive—how does expending energy lead to having more of it? Yet, the body thrives on this very paradox. Physical activity stimulates the release of endorphins, known as the body's feel-good hormones, which elevate mood and energy. This isn't merely a temporary boost but a sustained surge that supports us through our daily tasks and challenges.

Moreover, exercise plays a pivotal role in weight management. It's a powerful tool in balancing calories consumed with calories burned, but its benefits extend well beyond simple arithmetic. Regular physical activity enhances metabolic rate, meaning the body becomes more efficient at using energy, even at rest. This metabolic adaptation aids not only in weight loss or maintenance but in overall body ensuring a healthier ratio of muscle to fat.

In sum, the spectrum of exercise benefits is broad and deeply impactful. It's not only about living longer but about enriching the life we live. Through improved sleep, elevated energy levels, and better weight management, exercise fortifies our health, enabling us to lead fuller, more vibrant lives. It's a testament to the body's remarkable capacity for transformation and adaptation, a daily reminder of the resilience and strength that lies within us all.

Practical Tips and Techniques

Integrating Activity into Daily Routines

Start small. Oftentimes we want to dive straight in, stacking up daily exercise but then feeling let down when it becomes difficult to pursue. Don't stack your plate. Setting small, achievable goals to build the habit and then increasing the duration and intensity is ideal for long-term success.

A ten-minute walk multiple times a day can be a powerful starting point. Bonus points when you walk right after you have a meal; it makes it easier to digest alongside may help reduce blood sugar, help regulate blood pressure, and can help form a powerful habit.

You can incorporate movement breaks throughout your day. It's suggested to have five to ten minutes of movement per hour of inactivity. This can take the form of stretching, walking around for a bit, minor cleaning, or however you want it to take form. What works best is what works for you.

Exercise can have a wide range of meanings. Oftentimes it brings up "running, lifting, stretching, using a gym," and while those are perfectly fine and have great value if it works for you, you can play soccer or tennis instead of running. You can attend a yoga class, dance, or practice gymnastics. Lifting can be done at many jobs: farm work, calisthenics, or done outdoors.

It's best to identify the areas you want to work on and trace back activities you truly enjoy. I tend to exercise out of a gym in nature, whether it's my backyard or a park. I'm fortunate to have calisthenics equipment at many of my local parks, and you may as well.

Overcoming Common Barriers

The perception of not having enough time is a tried-and-true limiting belief. Oftentimes it boils down to prioritization. We can find time for many of our habits that may not be serving us how we like, yet keep us comfortable, but the moment we need to spend time on something that aligns with where we want to go, we have no time to pursue it!

Viewing physical activity as a non-negotiable of your day, akin to sleeping or eating, can help transform your approach. Here are some ways we can get past this mindset.

- Schedule Workouts: Block out a time that works best for you in your schedule, one that you know you can achieve and will create the least amount of effort to fulfill. A brand new 5 a.m. hour-long session every day may not be the best option.
- Combine Activities: Engaging in hobbies or sports with friends that achieve fitness goals is a fantastic way to get in activity without even feeling like you are. Alternatively, you can walk or cycle to the store, gym, work or park, rather than taking transportation.
- Time Audit: Spend a day (or week) writing down everything you do each day, from eating, Netflix, working out, etc. Is there anywhere you can reduce some time from activities that aren't serving you to add in time for activities that do?

Overcoming Fatigue

The next common excuse we get too is being too tired to work out or not having enough energy. It's interesting because our body will adapt to the environment. Not only does exercise help enhance our energy but our body will ramp itself up, making us feel more awake while we exercise. On the contrary, if you're inactive and wonder why you may be tired, your body is literally reducing the resources you need, slowing down your heart rate and many other functions, which keeps you in a more relaxed state.

The key is to start small and allow your body to adjust.

- Begin with Low-Intensity Activities: If fatigue is your issue, try a short walk, gentle yoga, or other, less demanding activities. These can invigorate your body without overwhelming it.
- Exercise at Your Peak Energy Times: Everyone's body is different. We have varying times that our energy peaks. For some it's the morning, while others find it in the afternoon or night. Identify the time that you have the most energy while also being able to exercise and aim for that.

Listening to Your Body

We may have a routine or mindset that is causing us to push our bodies, causing pain and discomfort. It's important to recognize our body's signals so we do not contribute to burnout or injury. This can greatly derail your fitness journey and lead to large lapses in time where we choose to no longer push forward in our goals.

- Adjust Your Routine as Needed: Be flexible with your exercise plan. If you feel particularly fatigued or sore, it may be a signal that you need an extra day or two of rest or a gentler workout.
- Seek Enjoyable Forms of Exercise: As mentioned earlier, find a form of exercise you truly enjoy. Experiment with different forms of exercise and make it something to look forward too rather than dread.
  - o As a side story, I absolutely disliked and hated the gym when I first started going years ago. I was embarrassed to even show up, felt weak, judged, and

incapable being in this new space. Each day I'd practically force myself out with my friend who encouraged me, and every day, I felt great afterwards. Over time, I grew to not only enjoy the gym, but have it be a genuine space for me to express myself, work through thoughts, and make progress in the direction I want to go in. Everything can change if you allow it the space to.

There are other ways you can support your fitness journey, such as:

- Set Realistic Goals: Having clear realistic goals such as losing weight, improving strength, or just being more active can have a huge influence over your motivation in going.
- Choose a Convenient Location: Regardless of where you exercise, make it as easy to get to as possible, whether it's a park, gym nearby, or a walk around your neighborhood.
- Find a Workout Buddy: Going with a friend was one of the most helpful things I've ever done when accomplishing fitness goals. It's harder to skip a workout when you're in a routine with someone else and can hold each other accountable.
- Join a Class: This is a great option if you want to show up and follow along with the class rather than have to do all the work yourself on what to exercise. I personally find class experiences to be helpful in not needing to think so hard on what's next but rather getting into the flow with like-minded individuals. This is also a good way to meet people who are aligned in the same direction as you.
- Reward Yourself: If you're putting in the work, give yourself a treat! For me this is getting delicious food, but it can also be watching TV, reading a book, or whatever you enjoy.

Exercise, in conclusion, is a habit that has immense transformational power on our physical body, mental health, spirit, and helps mitigate all causes of mortality, chronic diseases, anxiety, and depression alongside so many other benefits. It's something you can pick up and see results from a ten-minute walk to daily lifting or a well-planned-out program.

If your goal is to create your most aligned life, then it's time to start building and creating harmony in your body.

Nutrition: Nourishing the Body and Mind

The saying, "You are what you eat," is not only true but also concerning, considering that not all foods are created equal. On one side of the spectrum, we have ultra-processed foods, laden with toxic ingredients, presented by large food companies focused more on how to make a cheap product that resembles food. On the other, we have whole, organic foods with minimal processing, as nature intends. Typically grown locally, there are many small businesses sprouting out, offering high-quality goods.

What we eat significantly influences chronic illnesses, diseases, energy levels, cognition, gut flora, and practically every other aspect of our bodies. You may not be sick; you may be consuming low-quality food. Many people go about their day unaware of the critical importance of nutrition. Without proper nutrition, a multitude of problems will begin to manifest.

In this chapter, we won't be discussing any specific diets. Instead, we will offer general guidelines and useful information to help you make more informed choices regarding your personal food selections. For instance, ultra-processed foods accounted for sixty percent of the calories consumed from 2007 to 2012 (Baraldi et al., 2018). Additionally, from 2001 to 2018, there has been an increase in the consumption of an ultra-processed diet among Americans (Juul et al., 2022).

The Standard American Diet (SAD) notably increases risk factors to various illnesses, such as obesity, Type 2 diabetes, and cardiovascular disease. How can we maintain balance and alignment if the food we consume makes us feel sluggish or leads to chronic illness? We will delve into how organic foods can promote harmony within our bodies, providing the nutrition needed for a long and healthy life, as well as the many dangers of ultra-processed foods. The goal is to enable you to make more informed decisions about what you're eating, offering numerous tips along the way.

The Value of Organic and Locally Sourced Foods

Let's define what organic food is. Organic foods are grown and processed to specific standards that will vary by country but generally will include prohibitions against synthetic fertilizers, pesticides, and genetically modified organisms (GMO). In the United States, the USDA (Department of Agriculture) certifies organic foods as those grown in soil that has no prohibited substances applied for over three years prior to harvest.

When it comes to animal products, the USDA will certify only if the animal is living in conditions that accommodate their natural behavior (grazing on a pasture), that it is fed one hundred percent organic feed and forage, and not administered any antibiotics or hormones.

Unlike industrial farmed non-organic meats that are being fed GMO feed sprayed with herbicides such as glyphosate that make it into the cow and into you, organically raised animals receive natural feed, reducing your exposure to harmful chemicals and supporting healthier ecosystems. An article by the *Guardian* points to a report by the CDC showing that eighty percent of urine samples from children and adults had glyphosate in it, an herbicide linked to cancer as well (Gillam, 2022).

The USDA regulations on multi-ingredient processed foods prohibit it from having artificial preservatives, colors, or flavors and require the ingredients to be organic.

There are many benefits of organic foods which I'll list below:

- Higher Nutrient Levels: Organic foods often contain high levels of certain nutrients, including antioxidants and vitamins. Studies, like this one published in the *British Journal of Nutrition,* have found organic crops can have higher levels of antioxidants compared to non-organic foods. This may have reduced risk factors from both risk factors of having & getting a chronic disease (Barański et al., 2014).
- Lower Pesticide Residues: The very same studies show that organic produce is less likely to have pesticide residues. It noted that pesticide residue can be up to four times higher in conventional crops than their organic counterparts. Organic farming restricts the use of synthetic pesticides which gives us cleaner, healthier crops (Barański et al., 2014).
- Reduction in Toxic Heavy Metals: Organic crops have been shown to have a reduction in cadmium concentration, which is a toxic heavy metal. This is significant as exposure and consumption overtime can lead to many health problems (Barański et al., 2014).
- Environmental Benefits: When the land isn't being sprayed with toxic chemicals that leak into everything around it, you'd be surprised how life can flourish. By avoiding synthetic

fertilizers and pesticides, farmers are promoting biodiversity and ecological balance.

- Animal Welfare: Organic farms tend to have healthier standards of living for their animals compared to conventional industrial farms, including access to outdoor space and organic feed, which leads to happier animals. When we eat non-organic meats, we are eating sad, unhealthy animals that get slaughtered in cruel and unusual ways. There are many documentaries out there that will show you inside videos of how these animals are treated, which I highly recommend watching if you have a strong heart and soul. Trigger warning: they show some of the most brutal and inhumane ways industrial farms treat their animals.
- Fresher Produce: As the produce aren't filled with preservatives that will make them last a lifetime, you will often find organic foods are sourced closer to stores, making the produce fresher. Rather than arriving on boats months after being harvested, somehow keeping their appearance while being filled with juicy, delicious pesticides.

Locally sourced foods are my next recommendation. Oftentimes, as mentioned, they offer fresher produce in the shorter time between harvest and consumption, supporting not only better taste and nutrient preservation but also supporting the local economy and sustainability. This also contributes to a reduction in the carbon footprint compared to practices that involve long transportations routes.

It's also a great way to make some friends who have similar values by making friends at the local market or farm. Regardless, there are many benefits to sourcing local organic foods from their impact on health, the environment, and local communities.

The Dangers of Ultra-Processed Foods

Ultra-processed foods can be categorized by their extensive industrial processing and formulation. Ultimately, they belong more in a lab than they do in the kitchen, often containing many ingredients that are not typically used in home cooking. They are recognizable by their high amounts of added sugars, unhealthy fats, salt, artificial colors, flavors, and preservatives. A common example of this would be the frozen meals, packaged snacks, reconstituted meats, and soft drinks. Typically, these are cheaper, convenient, and quite literally have scientists make sure they're as addictive as they are delicious.

Not only this, but they boast an amazing shelf life. I'm sure you can look up on the internet the man who kept his McDonald's cheeseburger sitting on his counter to see how long it would last. I believe it's over ten years now, and it looks exactly the same. If they last so long on the shelf, I wonder how long they would last in your digestive system and how that may affect your gut lining or cause leaky gut syndrome. Joy.

Now onto the shady part, which is that these foods have ingredients that are harmful for anyone. The EU downright limited or banned these. Yet back home in the USA, the FDA still gives them a pass. For instance, certain artificial food dyes, preservatives like butylated hydroxy anisole (BHA) and butylated hydroxytoluene (BHT), and hydrogenated fats, which are sources of trans fats, have been linked to adverse health effects, including increased risk of cancer, heart disease, and behavioral issues in children.

Understanding what's in your food and the regulatory practice is essential when trying to protect yourself, family, or friends from harmful ingredients. Many of these ingredients, when eaten regularly, have long-term health consequences, such as endocrine disruption and increased chance of getting a chronic illness.

Eating ultra-processed foods leads to a wide array of negative health outcomes. They're high in calories, sugars, fats and low in nutrients. These foods can contribute to weight gain, obesity, factors closely related to the development of diabetes, heart disease, and certain cancers. Often, we overeat these products, yet without the nutrients, our bodies still aren't getting what they need.

The lack of nutrients can lead to imbalances in the body and affect overall health and well-being. The additives and artificial ingredients are also fantastic at disrupting your gut microbiome, which has a huge impact on many bodily functions alongside your mental health, contributing to gastrointestinal issues and possibly impacting immune function.

Some other ingredients that are banned abroad but not in the US are:

- Propylparaben: Banned in the EU for food and cosmetics due to its potential to disrupt sex hormones and sperm counts, with links to breast cancer.
- BHA and BHT: Synthetic antioxidants used in cereals and dehydrated foods, considered possible carcinogens and banned in the EU for their potential endocrine-disrupting effects.
- Synthetic Food Dyes (Blue 2, Yellow 5, Red 40): Used in beverages and candies, linked to tumors and hyperactivity in children, banned in Europe and Australia, which prefer natural colorings.
- GMOs: Widely accepted in the US but face bans or regulations in many European countries over safety concerns, especially related to glyphosate, a cancer-linked herbicide used with GMO crops.

- Roxarsone: An arsenic-based drug previously used in chicken feed, not officially banned in the US but linked to cancer and birth defects, leading to its EU ban.
- Ractopamine: A muscle enhancer for livestock, banned in over 122 countries due to reproductive and cardiovascular health risks but still used in the US.

The widespread availability and aggressive marketing of ultra-processed foods, coupled with their addictive qualities—primarily due to high sugar and fat content—pose significant challenges to public health. Recognizing the dangers of these foods is a crucial step toward making healthier dietary choices and advocating for policies that prioritize the well-being of consumers over industrial food production interests.

Water Quality

Water is one of the most crucial aspects to a well-functioning body. It's found that even two to three percent loss of body weight (water), being a low to mild dehydration, can reduce cognitive functioning, mood, short-term memory, and attention. Besides this, the quality of your water has a huge impact on how it hydrates you or causes detriment.

As with food, there are varying levels of quality you can have with water, whether that be the lower spectrum, tap water, plastic bottled water (has massive levels of micro plastics) and other contaminated sources that wreak havoc on our bodies, or high-quality spring water, alkaline, hydrogen, or reverse osmosis water, each having their own benefits on the body.

High-Quality Spring Water

- Natural Filtration: Spring water is naturally filtered through rocks, which enriches it with beneficial minerals like calcium, magnesium, and potassium.

- Pure and Clean: It is typically free from many of the contaminants found in tap water due to its protected underground source.
- pH Balanced: Spring water is naturally balanced in pH, which can help maintain the body's acid-base balance.

Alkaline Water

- pH Level: Alkaline water has a higher pH level compared to regular drinking water. This can help neutralize the acid in your bloodstream.
- Antioxidant Properties: It may contain antioxidant properties that help to prevent the growth of cell-damaging free radicals in the body, potentially slowing the aging process.
- Hydration and Digestion: It can improve hydration and aid digestion. Some studies suggest it might help with reducing acid reflux.

Hydrogen Water

- Antioxidant Benefits: Hydrogen water contains molecular hydrogen, which is an effective antioxidant. It helps fight oxidative stress and inflammation, which are linked to various diseases.
- Enhanced Energy: The molecular hydrogen in hydrogen water may help to improve energy levels by making the body's energy production more efficient.
- Improved Athletic Performance: Some evidence suggests that hydrogen water can reduce muscle fatigue and inflammation after exercise, potentially improving athletic performance.

Reverse Osmosis Water

- Purity: Reverse osmosis water is highly purified, removing contaminants such as pesticides, bacteria, and heavy metals.

- Taste: The purification process can improve the taste of water by removing impurities that can cause a bad taste or odor.
- Safe for Compromised Immune Systems: The level of purification makes it safe for individuals with compromised immune systems or for those who need the purest form of water.
- Remineralization: If you plan to drink it, it's a good idea to re-mineralize the water through another system or add in your own minerals and electrolytes, as all of that will be removed with the purification process.

Tap water itself is contaminated with many heavy metals, chlorines, fluoride, Atrazine, and other substances which are found in "legal" levels but legal does not mean safe. In fact, most tap water is found to have unsafe levels of contamination. If you're curious to know what your tap is like, check out ewg.org/tapwater. You can input your zip code and find out how safe your water is.

If all you did was change your water source to be high-quality, stored in glass, spring water alongside keeping yourself properly hydrated throughout your day, you would find massive benefits all around for your mood and physiology. With this, you can also have the metaphysical elements of water.

Water holds the vibrational frequency that is projected onto it. A study done by Masaru Emoto found that by projecting different energy at water can change the molecular structure of it. Water that had positive affirmations projected at it had a beautiful, symmetrical structure. Negative projection had a more destructive molecular structure.

This makes me wonder if it sheds light on why so many religions and cultures blessed their food and water before consuming it. I mean, haven't we all heard how good food tastes when someone really puts their love into it?

Regardless, by sourcing high-quality water, stored in glass bottles along with adopting better habits around hydration, you will notice a massive shift in your own body and mental state.

Here are some tips you can utilize for getting the most out of your water:

- Hydrate consistently throughout the day. Have smaller sips more frequently (every hour) rather than a large quantity once you feel dehydrated or thirsty.
- Source high-quality spring water or find a spring near you. If you do find a spring, make sure you test the water for contaminants. https://findaspring.org/ is a great source to find a spring nearby.
- Use glass containers for storage. I personally love the brand bluebottlelove.com, but any glass storage will work!
- Bless your water and send gratitude to it when you consume it. It's quite literally saving your life, after all. Without water, we would all perish!
- Use a shower filter! You can absorb contaminants through your largest organ: your skin! Using a shower filter can help catch all the nastiness in your own water and do wonders for your skin health.
  - Side note: You can also get a filter for under your sinks, or a whole house water filter. There are plenty of options you can find at a local hardware store or online. If you do choose to do this, get a reverse osmosis filter, which is the highest filtration quality. Also, be aware that it filters out the good minerals as well. If you drink reverse osmosis water, you need to make sure you have a system that will re-mineralize it. This can be done through you putting in mineral

powders and electrolytes or buying a system that does it for you under the sink.

- Use a simple electrolyte water recipe to utilize upon risings. The fact is, we're dehydrated when we wake up. You may not be tired, but rather heavily dehydrated. It's best to consume a full glass of water with electrolytes.
  - o Recipe:
    - Full glass of water (16oz)
    - Lemon or lime squeezed into it
    - A pinch of sea salt (I prefer Redmond, or Celtic Salt)

Simple Dietary Guidelines and Tips

- Check Out the Dirty Dozen: These are fruits and vegetables rated by the EWG (Environmental Working Group) as having the most pesticide residue. Prioritizing these for organic purchase can be a good starting point.
- Prioritize Whole Foods: Eat whole foods as much as possible, whether that's meat or produce. Limit as much processed foods as you can. If you go into a grocery store, you will find they all have the same layout. The edges of the store will always be whole foods, (fruits, vegetables, meats), while the center with all the aisles will hold the processed foods.
- Read Labels: Understanding and learning how to read food labels is incredibly beneficial to know what you're eating. There are many videos online or books that explain this. I also quite enjoy using an app called Fooducate. It will scan the barcode of your food and then list all the ingredients and if they're harmful or not.

- Incorporate Organic or Local Foods: Do your best to shop organic and buy local. I always go by the rule of getting the best you can with the resources you have.
- Limit Calories from Added Sugars: You will find once you start looking at added sugars, companies love to shove as many as they can into a product. Do your best to avoid added sugars and to get your sugar from whole-food sources such as fruit.
- Focus on Variety, Nutrient Density, and Amount: One of the key guidelines from the US government is to have variety on our plates, something I can agree with. Humans from the beginning of time have never always had one specific type of food. They ate a variety of plants, meat, or whatever they had on hand, and I tend to eat the same way. What's best is understanding what diet works for you and for your specific goals and values. Always opt for higher-quality nutrient-dense foods.

Sleep Hygiene

We all know what it's like to miss out on a night of sleep. Without getting a proper night of rest, we become groggy, tired, unmotivated, and rely heavier on caffeine or other supplements to make it through our day. Whether you're staying up late, or the quality of your sleep is poor, sleep is critical to our overall health and wellness.

Adults who have less than seven hours of sleep have an increased risk of depression, anxiety, heart attack, asthma, and stroke. Lack of sleep can also contribute to unhealthy weight gain, Type 2 diabetes, and high blood pressure.

Regardless of the downfalls of sleepless nights, in order to live in harmony with your body and have maximum success towards staying focused and staying in alignment with the highest version of yourself, you'll have to master the art of sleeping.

There are many ways you can support yourself in having the proper amount and quality of sleep regardless of your situation, many of which are very simple to implement, and that's what this whole subsection is about.

Let's stop making it harder for ourselves with habits that no longer serve us and take a good hard look at our sleeping patterns.

Benefits of Sleep Hygiene

As you may imagine, sleep isn't only about getting a solid night's rest. It's intricately connected to our health and overall well-being. When we get an adequate amount of REM sleep with high-quality sleep, we receive many benefits. A good night's rest can help us process our memories on a deeper level, support our hormone production, enhance cognitive functioning, bolster our immune system, and support our mental health and well-being. I know I'm not alone in feeling quite poorly after a restless night, which leads into the actions I do or do not take the next day.

Proper Sleep Environment

Where you're sleeping has a major impact on the quality of your sleep and how easy it is to get to bed. There are many ways you can create a relaxing environment for the bedroom, the tips below can help give you ideas on where you can start.

- Maintain a Comfortable Temperature: Humans sleep best between sixty to sixty-seven degrees. This helps facilitate the natural drop in temperature that occurs when we fall asleep.
- Set up your bedroom to be a place of relaxation and sleep. If you have a computer in there to work on, your brain will

automatically adjust to seeing this as a place of work. Each time you try going to sleep, your brain will focus on what you do in this space such as working. To avoid this, be intentional with how you use your space.

- Reduce Noise: Minimize the amount of noise with heavy curtains, soundproofing the room, double-paned windows, or incorporating a white noise machine that helps block our disruptive sounds. You could also try earplugs.

- Limit Light Exposure: Light is the absolute killer of sleep. Light itself is a signal that it is daytime and you're ready to keep going. We sleep best in pitch-black. Even a pinhole of light can be disruptive to sleep, especially blue lights. Avoid blue light at all costs! You can utilize blackout curtains alongside using a sleep mask. I was opposed to the sleep mask for many years and once I found one that was comfortable and made myself sleep with it, I could never think about sleeping without one again.

- Invest in a Quality Mattress, Pillows, and Bedding: Many of us spend our money on things we will use once and toss away, yet where we sleep is something we use every single night. Invest in a high-quality sleeping environment, prioritizing one hundred percent organic cotton or linen bedding, down comforter, and an organic mattress. While these are on the higher end, it's important to do your best with what you can afford and upgrade when it's in alignment.

- Minimize EMFs: Electromagnetic frequencies have a major impact on your health and especially your sleep quality. Put your phone on airplane mode and keep it at least ten to fifteen feet away from your body or in a faraday bag. You can consider having your router be connected to an automatic timer (or unplug before bed), so the Wi-Fi isn't disrupting your own electromagnetic field. It's great because you're sleeping, so there's no need for it to be on anyways.

- Maintain a Clutter-Free Environment: Clean up, boss! Nothing is more distracting than coming into your space to sleep and seeing a mess of chores you need to tackle. Clutter in your environment, as discussed, creates clutter in your mind.

- Incorporate a Calming Scent: Utilize a diffuser to blast you to sleep with the calming effects of lavender or chamomile. If you do this regularly with the same scent, your mind will automatically adjust to being in a state of sleep easier by smelling the aroma, along with the effects of the oil you use.

Regardless of what your current situation is, you can utilize one or all of these simple tips to help you create a proper environment for restful sleep. Not only this, but if you're bringing a date home or trying to impress your partner, keep your bedroom looking fresh and ready to rumble.

The next section will include some more general tips, but before that, I want to stress something of great importance. Make sleep a ritual—cherish your sleep! Creating a sleep routine for yourself is one the best things you can do. Make it unique to what you genuinely enjoy and allows you to easily get into a state of relaxation. Below will be techniques you can incorporate into a sleep-time routine alongside having proper sleep hygiene.

- Morning or Afternoon Light: The best light you can receive is when the sun is rising and when the sun is setting. This will help support your natural circadian rhythm alongside giving you beautiful red-light frequencies that help increase cellular energy.

- Limit Caffeine Intake: Do your best to drink your caffeine sixty to ninety minutes after waking. Limit or stop drinking caffeine after boon. Caffeine's half-life is typically five to six hours, meaning if you drink 200 mg of caffeine at noon, at 6 p.m. you'll have 100 mg still in your system and 50 mg at midnight. Any amount of caffeine in your system while going to sleep can reduce your sleep quality, alongside making it difficult to get to sleep.

- Limit Bright Light Exposure at Night: Keeping the lights dim in your home when the sun goes down is a great way to help your body know it's time to start winding down. Red light can also be utilized as it mimics the light you can receive at sunset, has a low impact on melatonin production, and reduces eye strain. It'll help your body get into a natural rhythm, potentially making it easier to get a restful night's sleep.

- Avoid Blue Light: Blue light keeps us awake and will actively hurt our melatonin production. We receive this from any screens we see or artificial lighting we may have on.
    - Use blue block glasses.
    - Utilize a program such as F.lux for your computer screen.
    - Use night mode on your phone or turn on your phone's grayscale or red-light option when the sun goes down.

- Stop Eating Two to Three Hours Before Bed: When your body is actively digesting, it makes it more difficult to get into a deep sleep. If you have a large dinner, try to do it two to three hours before bed. It's alright to have a small snack if hunger will keep you up before bed, but if it's heavy in sugar, it'll have a negative impact on sleep.

- Exercise Daily: Exercise is a huge help to many areas, including sleep. Daily exercise will help you fall asleep easier and get a more restful night of deep sleep.
- Meditation, Visualization, or Mindfulness Practice: The best time to reprogram your subconscious is when you wake up and right before going to sleep. You can use this time to relax, reprogram and sleep deep. (Often, my nighttime meditation leads me directly into falling asleep and is a win-win in my book)
- Stick to a Sleep Schedule: Going to bed and waking up at the same time will help strengthen your circadian rhythm to make it easier to get deep sleep.
- Limit Alcohol Intake: Many find solace in alcohol's relaxing effects, and while it can be easier to help you get to sleep, it disrupts our ability to get into REM, which is our deep sleep. Oftentimes, you may sleep for seven to ten hours and feel as if you had no sleep at all.
- Utilize a Nighttime (Non-Alcoholic) Cocktail or Supplements: One of my favorite parts of my routine is making my nighttime tea, which is an organic sleep-time blend of herbs. Utilizing our plant friends, we can make a delicious treat and ease us into relaxation and sleep.

Important Note: Always consult a healthcare professional before taking any supplements. You are responsible for your health and awareness around what you consume. Many herbs or supplements can have contraindications towards medications, chronic illnesses or disease, or pregnancy.

- Sleepy-Time Tea Blend: passionflower, chamomile, spearmint, lemon balm, lemon grass, valerian root.

- ⊛ Tart Cherry Juice: This can help give you natural melatonin production. Make sure it's organic, has no added sugar, and is purely tart cherry juice with no additives. (I have to hide it because it's so damn delicious my wife will drink the whole dang thing)

- ⊛ Magnesium, Magnesium, Magnesium: Fun fact—over half the population of the United States was found to have a magnesium deficiency. Magnesium has many benefits and is a cofactor for over three hundred enzymatic reactions. It can help with energy production, muscle movement, nervous system regulation, electrolyte balance, and so much more. Magnesium can also help us get into a state of relaxation and fall asleep. I personally buy the brand from Bioptimizers that has seven different forms of bioavailable magnesium, but I recommend doing your own research and finding what works for you. What matters most is quality.
  - o Magnesium Threonate specifically helps with winding down and getting a good night's rest.

- ⊛ Listen to a Sleep Podcast: If you're a fan of podcasts, I absolutely recommend giving Andrew Huberman a try. He has multiple stellar podcasts that go deeper into sleep hygiene at a very high level yet convey information in a way anyone can utilize.

In conclusion, sleep plays a pivotal role in maintaining our physiological health, mental well-being, and daily functionality. By focusing on improving our sleep hygiene, we can create a harmonious environment that supports our ability to progress in our tasks and maintain balance in our lives. I encourage you to actively engage with and have fun exploring the sleep improvement strategies discussed. Experiment with the tips provided to discover what works for you and tailor your own routine accordingly. Embrace this journey of personalization; as you fine-tune your sleep habits, you will likely notice significant enhancements in your overall quality of life. Remember, the goal is not just to change how you sleep, but to transform how you feel, think, and operate day-to-day.

What lies behind us and what lies before us are tiny matters compared to what lies within us.

- RALPH WALDO EMERSON

12

The Final Notes

If you made it this far, I hope you've been able to find the wisdom and techniques I've shared useful and able to incorporate them into your life in a positive way. I'm truly grateful for not only supporting you but being of service to you in any form that I could. The goal of this book was to give you a baseline of tools and frameworks that can get the ball rolling in your court, taking back your power and discovering the unique light you have to offer. If I've been able to do just a fraction of that, I've succeeded in my mission. Of course, I also hope you've been able to see who I am and the style I bring with me in my coaching frameworks and to be able to work with anyone who feels called to go deeper into this journey.

I'll be leaving you with three of the top tips I have for you in order to have as much success as possible with incorporating and applying these techniques in your life.

Tip #1: Own Your Personal Responsibility and Take Back Your Power

The moment we become victims to our circumstances, blaming others or events that may have occurred, we give away our power. We tell ourselves and the universe at whole that we are not the co-creators of our destiny, we do not create our reality, and there is nothing we can do about it. We allow life to happen to us, rather than taking hold of the reins to steer around or gain lessons from our circumstances.

This is a faulty mindset, and while there are events we cannot control in our lives, we can control how we react and move forward from these events. Once we recognize our own part in the patterns, we cultivate that do not serve us, and then take intentional action towards reversing or halting those patterns, we regain control of our lives.

How we react and the patterns we cultivate ultimately lead into the person we become, for better or worse. We are not a stagnant human who is "born like this," "always unlucky," etc., but we can utilize intentional action to guide us into the person we truly are and always meant to be.

Tip #2: Setbacks and Challenges Are Lessons

Regardless of where we are in our life, we are not bound to keeping things the same. We are never stuck, whether you feel like you've messed up your life every year since birth or inevitably falling into the wrong direction... We can do something about it. Every single setback you've ever had can either continue to be just that, or you can extract the wisdom out of it. What can you learn? What can you do differently? How can you avoid the same outcome in the future? The more challenging situations you've been through, the more wisdom you have to gain regardless of if it was something that hurt you or was positive in your life.

Setbacks are inevitable, and I've had many writing this book. The only reason why I finished this book is because I kept going regardless of what the circumstances were, how long I may have taken in between chapters, or the emotions I felt sharing who I am and what I have to offer to the world at large. One part grateful for the impact it may have in the lives of others and my own, one part scared of being vulnerable and the judgment that may occur.

You will be rewarded for pushing past the fear of the unknown and grateful for the lessons you receive from doing so.

Setbacks only affect us when we quit, when we choose to say we aren't meant for this, this is a sign that we shouldn't have tried, or fall back into a victim mentality. Yet when we see challenges from a growth-based mindset, we know this is not true but a massive limiting belief. Setbacks and challenges allow us to one, siphon the wisdom from the situation, and two, allow us to put into practice everything we've learned and cultivated.

They're milestones to show the universe we are ready to move beyond and choose differently rather than stay stagnant and revert back to the person we are actively trying to grow out of.

Tip #3: Abundance, Success, and Wealth Are Always Present

We do not gain abundance. It is not a mystical teaching we must learn to tap into. We never "lack" any of these aspects; rather we must hold space for allowing it to come freely to us. Abundance, success, and wealth, however you may define it, is a presence that is always here and accessible to all. It is our mindsets, thoughtforms, and patterns that create the separation we feel from these aspects; we ourselves create the barriers that do not allow these energies to cultivate within our lives.

These aspects are uniquely created by the definitions and thoughts we hold of them. How you choose to define wealth will greatly affect how you cultivate it. Wealth, abundance, and success to me is being able to take any actions as I see fit without any major barriers, being able to choose experiences without it taking a massive toll on my current situation. Yet on a smaller scale, wealth is the ability to make choices that create that freedom, for we are always free. Abundance is being able to wake up and feel the sunshine on our skin. Success is being able to provide for my family whether it be small actions or large.

We can tap into these energies on every level of the spectrum and cultivate them through the way we choose to see them and allow them to run freely through us. What do these terms mean to you? How can you see them already present within your life? How can you cultivate a greater relationship with this energy that is already flowing that creates gratitude around it? You are the expert in your life and know more than anyone could about this.

What to Do Next

We've gone over the major frameworks and techniques, and I'll sum them up quickly for you:

Create a Crystal-Clear Vision

- Creating this vision, in the first person, as if it's already happened through many of the techniques I've listed and focusing on this, will allow your mind and actions to naturally adapt in that direction, connecting you to that future and pulling it into the now moment.
- Focus on your big why, for without a big enough mission, big enough why, it will be difficult to tap into the mindsets to push through the challenging aspects of this journey and to stay focused.
- A clear vision helps give us a glimpse of who you are becoming and what that life looks like.

Cultivate Positive Mindsets and Patterns that Bring Alignment into Your Life

- Identify what no longer serves you and create a plan around the techniques I've mentioned to shift your mindset to one that allows abundance to flow in your most aligned life.
- See challenges and setbacks as a perfect situation to practice your newfound skills.

Identify the Limiting Beliefs and Negative Aspects of the Self

- You will encounter limiting beliefs, and the challenges that arise from walking in your own truth and aligned life will no doubt shed light on the more unsavory aspects of our being.
- Make friends with your shadow, understand it, have gratitude for it, and use it as a tool to gain deep insight into your own life. Start to heal these wounds to step into the person you always had within you. The person who is in the future, cheering you on for moving beyond these patterns and grateful for the work you put in.

Utilize the Power of Universal Magic, Baby

- There are many techniques, tools, and universal laws that are here to support you or be a part of your downfall (dun dun dunnn).
- Your energy is sacred. Feed it, understand it, and cultivate it to collaborate with you, rather than against you.
- Align your thoughts with intentional actions and strong emotions to literally manifest your ideal reality through the law of attraction.
- Create powerful boundaries and energetic spaces that help support your journey rather than being another thing taking up space in your mind,

Shift Your Internal State and Find Relaxation with Breathwork and Meditation

- Using these powerful tools in conjunction with the lessons learned in this book will have a major impact on your success.
- If all you did was start a regular meditation practice, you'd gain so much wisdom, insight, stress relief, and confidence in your own life. I invite you to do just that.

Take Care of Your Body and Bring It to a State of Harmony

- When we are aware of how we treat our bodies, we start to recognize that exercise, sleep, and nutrition are acts of self-care.
- By fueling and bringing balance to the body, you make it easier to achieve every aspect of what you are manifesting and becoming.
- Small steps go a long way to supporting your needs.

The very first and most important step you can take is understanding the direction you want to go. There's absolutely no need to know the path, for that is unknown and often will surprise you as it unfolds like a beautiful novel—*your* unique novel, at that. The sooner you can create an absolutely crystal-clear vision and end point for what you're creating, the quicker you will begin to pull that future into the now moment.

Take a small actionable step and create that vision if it's all you do.

If you feel called to go deeper with someone who has been through it and now actively works towards helping others, I invite you to book a free call with yours truly. From custom action plans, to working through limiting beliefs and doing the work with you step by step, that's exactly what I offer through my business. Go to mightywellness.us/schedule to book a call.

Letter to the Reader

As you may already know, my name is Anthony Emilo. I grew up in San Diego, California, and throughout my life, I was challenged. It all began when I started elementary with a beautiful lisp that caused every damn word out of my mouth to be "unique," yet many people found it amusing, which led to bullying. In fact, I'm quite comfortable and glad that this was the case, for without these circumstances, I likely wouldn't be on the path I am writing this book. For me though, this meant having a dislike of being around others alongside deep self-loathing for myself. I couldn't speak without garnering some form of negative attention.

From here, I retreated from the world and became obsessed with video games, another habit that I have healthy boundaries with today, yet at the time it consumed every ounce of my being. It allowed me to find friends in a way that was comfortable, some I still have with me today.

This ultimately led to having quite a bit of self-esteem issues, anxiety, depression, and massive amounts of fear. Not being able to love myself or connect with others, nor having the wisdom or help at the time to break out of these patterns. Fortunately, in my later years, I moved away.

Yet this experience of moving out of the city and to the high desert when I was sixteen also gave me a space to truly be with myself, with minimal influence from the outside world. Through what I believe are synchronicities that were destined to happen, which I'll explain in a bit, I started down a spiritual path to re-aligning with who I truly discovering so many aspects I thought made me "weird" as massive strengths that I actively use today.

It was truly divine alignment that led me here, for so many years I felt trapped and depressed, more so than I've ever felt. Each day I was met with a worsening condition, imagining my demise throughout the day. At that time, I didn't have the best quality of sleep (and it showed). Typically, I'd wake up and immediately be met with my negative mind, swirling around in despair, unable to go back to sleep, and so I'd lie in bed until morning.

Yet one night I was struck, waking up in a panic, and I couldn't stop this intense feeling that I had to go on my computer. I could not go back to sleep. As I got up and worked my way over, I sought out knowledge in an unexpected corner of the internet, a notorious hub for digital hermits.

In the depths of this online hellscape, the very first thing I saw was a video that led me to a man who was giving a speech on how humans are light beings, inhabiting a physical vessel in this universal school. Through this hour-long presentation, I resonated so deeply, my entire body began to vibrate intensely. I couldn't stop this feeling of immense truth unlocking through my body and out the crown of my head. I had no idea what this meant and why it was happening, just that somehow, some way I needed to go deeper into this field of research.

I was already quite acquainted to learning about the harmful aspects of our world, the lies being told by those we should trust most, the poison in our foods, the lack of education in our educational system, and the full-fledged war on consciousness to keep folks stuck in a constant state of survival, never able to move beyond or even question how things could be different.

While this newfound field of knowledge, ancient wisdom, subconscious reprogramming, universal laws, and a new way to see this world around me began to unfold, I learned how to meditate, reach altered states of consciousness, made constant effort to learn how to remote view and astral project, alongside other ancient teachings. This led me into a state of how to reverse my limiting patterns.

From that moment forward, I knew I had a mission to change my life. I had deep feelings of knowing I would make change in the world, help others, somehow, some way. But I simply did not have the vessel, insight, or vehicle to do so yet. In fact, I was an incredibly sheltered, New Age dork who could barely talk to anyone. Yet over many other synchronicities, I can now see the entire path unfolding before my eyes, how each event in my past led to this very moment and how this moment is the beginning of my own becoming story.

Now I am choosing to share my story, knowledge, and tools that have helped me with anyone who resonates and finds my work. I genuinely hope you have gained a deeper insight into yourself and begin on this path, as I did and as we all eventually will.

Thank you so much for supporting me as I grow this business. I will continue creating this path and sharing it with others!

I do not take this journey lightly and will constantly continue to grow and learn to be of service to others to the best of my own ability.

Much love,

Anthony Emilo

References

Dijkstra, N., & Fleming, S. M. (2023). Subjective signal strength distinguishes reality from imagination. *Nature Communications, 14*(1). https://doi.org/10.1038/s41467-023-37322-1

Dweck, C. S. (2007). *Mindset the new pscyhology of Success.* Ballantine.

Eby, L. T., Allen, T. D., Evans, S. C., Ng, T., & DuBois, D. L. (2008). Does mentoring matter? A multidisciplinary meta-analysis comparing mentored and non-mentored individuals. *Journal of Vocational Behavior, 72*(2), 254–267. https://doi.org/10.1016/j.jvb.2007.04.005

Kilby, C. J., & Sherman, K. A. (2016). Delineating the relationship between stress mindset and primary appraisals: Preliminary findings. *SpringerPlus, 5*(1). https://doi.org/10.1186/s40064-016-1937-7

Smith, E. N., Young, M. D., & Crum, A. J. (2020). Stress, mindsets, and success in Navy seals special warfare training. *Frontiers in Psychology, 10.* https://doi.org/10.3389/fpsyg.2019.02962

Lee, L. O., James, P., Zevon, E. S., Kim, E. S., Trudel-Fitzgerald, C., Spiro, A., Grodstein, F., & Kubzansky, L. D. (2019). Optimism is associated with exceptional longevity in 2 epidemiologic cohorts of men and women. *Proceedings of the National Academy of Sciences, 116*(37), 18357–18362. https://doi.org/10.1073/pnas.1900712116

Segerstrom, S. C., & Sephton, S. E. (2010). Optimistic expectancies and cell-mediated immunity. *Psychological Science, 21*(3), 448–455. https://doi.org/10.1177/0956797610362061

Sansone, R. A., & Sansone, L. A. (2010, November). *Gratitude and well being: The benefits of Appreciation*. Psychiatry (Edgmont (Pa. : Township)). https://www.ncbi.nlm.nih.gov/pmc/articles/PMC3010965/

American Psychological Association. (2019, October 30). *Mindfulness meditation: A research-proven way to reduce stress*. American Psychological Association. https://www.apa.org/topics/mindfulness/meditation

da Silva, C. C., Bolognani, C. V., Amorim, F. F., & Imoto, A. M. (2023). Effectiveness of training programs based on mindfulness in reducing psychological distress and promoting well-being in medical students: A systematic review and meta-analysis. *Systematic Reviews, 12*(1). https://doi.org/10.1186/s13643-023-02244-y

Hoge, E. A., Bui, E., Mete, M., Dutton, M. A., Baker, A. W., & Simon, N. M. (2023). Mindfulness-based stress reduction vs Escitalopram for the treatment of adults with anxiety disorders. *JAMA Psychiatry, 80*(1), 13. https://doi.org/10.1001/jamapsychiatry.2022.3679

Balban, M. Y., Neri, E., Kogon, M. M., Weed, L., Nouriani, B., Jo, B., Holl, G., Zeitzer, J. M., Spiegel, D., & Huberman, A. D. (2023). Brief structured respiration practices enhance mood and reduce physiological arousal. *Cell Reports Medicine, 4*(1), 100895. https://doi.org/10.1016/j.xcrm.2022.100895

The impact of meditation on cognitive function. Better Aging. (2020, July 14). https://www.betteraging.com/aging-science/can-meditation-impact-age-related-cognitive-decline/

Malinowski   Reader in Cognitive Neuroscience, P. (2018, September 19). *Mindfulness meditation: Ten Minutes a day improves cognitive function*. The Conversation. https://theconversation.com/mindfulness-meditation-ten-minutes-a-day-improves-cognitive-function-103386#:~:text=Facebook,known%20as%20%E2%80%9Cworking%20memory

Mckeehan, N. (2020, January 29). *Meditation – its effect on cognition and general well-being*. Alzheimer's Drug Discovery Foundation. https://www.alzdiscovery.org/cognitive-vitality/blog/meditation-its-effect-on-cognition-and-general-well-being#:~:text=Some%20studies%20suggest%20that%20MBSR,cognition%20and%20reported%20mindfulness

Ziedman, E. (2022, May 11). *The benefits of mindfulness meditation for Cognitive Health and learni*. Chopra. https://chopra.com/blogs/meditation/the-benefits-of-mindfulness-meditation-for-cognitive-health-and-learning#:~:text=In%20mild%20cognitive%20impairment%20,

Dolan, E. W. (2023a, July 6). *Mindfulness meditation can improve motor control and selective attention, study finds*. PsyPost. https://www.psypost.org/mindfulness-meditation-can-improve-motor-control-and-selective-attention-study-finds/

Dolan, E. W. (2023b, September 28). *Mindfulness meditation might help people manage emotional distractions, new study suggests*. PsyPost. https://www.psypost.org/mindfulness-meditation-might-help-people-manage-emotional-distractions-new-study-suggests/#:~:text=Findings%20from%20a%20recent%20study,meditators

Hoge, E. A., Bui, E., Marques, L., Metcalf, C. A., Morris, L. K., Robinaugh, D. J., Worthington, J. J., Pollack, M. H., & Simon, N. M. (2013). Randomized controlled trial of mindfulness meditation for generalized anxiety disorder. *The Journal of Clinical Psychiatry*, 74(08), 786–792. https://doi.org/10.4088/jcp.12m08083

Woodcock, R. (2023, January 30). *The role of spirituality in mental well-being*. AACSB. https://www.aacsb.edu/insights/articles/2023/01/the-role-of-spirituality-in-mental-well-being

Marusak, H. (2023, January 26). *Meditation and mindfulness may be as effective as medication for treating certain mental conditions*. PsyPost. https://www.psypost.org/meditation-and-mindfulness-may-be-as-effective-as-medication-for-treating-certain-conditions/

Fincham, G. W., Strauss, C., Montero-Marin, J., & Cavanagh, K. (2023). Effect of breathwork on stress and mental health: A meta-analysis of randomised-controlled trials. *Scientific Reports, 13*(1). https://doi.org/10.1038/s41598-022-27247-y

Oschman, J., Chevalier, G., & Brown, R. (2015). The effects of grounding (earthing) on inflammation, the immune response, wound healing, and prevention and treatment of chronic inflammatory and autoimmune diseases. *Journal of Inflammation Research*, 83. https://doi.org/10.2147/jir.s69656

Chevalier, G., Sinatra, S. T., Oschman, J. L., & Delany, R. M. (2013). Earthing (grounding) the human body reduces blood viscosity— a major factor in cardiovascular disease. *The Journal of Alternative and Complementary Medicine, 19*(2), 102–110. https://doi.org/10.1089/acm.2011.0820

Sinatra, S. T., Sinatra, D. S., Sinatra, S. W., & Chevalier, G. (2022). Grounding – the universal anti-inflammatory remedy. *Biomedical Journal, 46*(1), 11–16. https://doi.org/10.1016/j.bj.2022.12.002

Ward, B. W., Schiller, J. S., & Goodman, R. A. (2014). Multiple chronic conditions among US adults: A 2012 update. *Preventing Chronic Disease, 11*. https://doi.org/10.5888/pcd11.130389

Liguory, G., Feito, Y., Fountaine, C., & Roy, B. A. (2022). *ACSM's guidelines for exercise testing and prescription*. Wolters Kluwer.

Singh, B., Olds, T., Curtis, R., Dumuid, D., Virgara, R., Watson, A., Szeto, K., O'Connor, E., Ferguson, T., Eglitis, E., Miatke, A., Simpson, C. E., & Maher, C. (2023, September 29). *Effectiveness of physical activity interventions for improving depression, anxiety and distress: An overview of systematic reviews*. British Journal of Sports Medicine. https://bjsm.bmj.com/content/57/18/1203

ERICKSON, K. I., HILLMAN, C., STILLMAN, C. M., BALLARD, R. M., BLOODGOOD, B., CONROY, D. E., MACKO, R., MARQUEZ, D.

X., PETRUZZELLO, S. J., & POWELL, K. E. (2019). Physical activity, cognition, and Brain Outcomes: A review of the 2018 physical activity guidelines. *Medicine & Science in Sports & Exercise, 51*(6), 1242–1251. https://doi.org/10.1249/mss.0000000000001936

Baraldi, L. G., Martinez Steele, E., Canella, D. S., & Monteiro, C. A. (2018). Consumption of ultra-processed foods and associated sociodemographic factors in the USA between 2007 and 2012: Evidence from a nationally representative cross-sectional study. *BMJ Open, 8*(3). https://doi.org/10.1136/bmjopen-2017-020574

Juul, F., Parekh, N., Martinez-Steele, E., Monteiro, C. A., & Chang, V. W. (2022). Ultra-processed food consumption among US adults from 2001 to 2018. *The American Journal of Clinical Nutrition, 115*(1), 211–221. https://doi.org/10.1093/ajcn/nqab305

Gillam, G. (2022, July 9). *"disturbing": Weedkiller ingredient tied to cancer found in 80% of us urine samples.* The Guardian. https://www.theguardian.com/us-news/2022/jul/09/weedkiller-glyphosate-cdc-study-urine-samples

Barański, M., Średnicka-Tober, D., Volakakis, N., Seal, C., Sanderson, R., Stewart, G. B., Benbrook, C., Biavati, B., Markellou, E., Giotis, C., Gromadzka-Ostrowska, J., Rembiałkowska, E., Skwarło-Sońta, K., Tahvonen, R., Janovská, D., Niggli, U., Nicot, P., & Leifert, C. (2014). Higher antioxidant and lower cadmium concentrations and lower incidence of pesticide residues in organically grown crops: A systematic literature review and meta-analyses. *British Journal of Nutrition, 112*(5), 794–811. https://doi.org/10.1017/s0007114514001366

www.ingramcontent.com/pod-product-compliance
Lightning Source LLC
Chambersburg PA
CBHW061743120626
46550CB00005B/1869